∞

The Spiritual Life

Fr. Jean Nicolas Grou

The Spiritual Life

A Comprehensive Manual for
Catholics Seeking Salvation

SOPHIA INSTITUTE PRESS®
Manchester, New Hampshire

The Spiritual Life is an abridged edition of *Manual for Interior Souls* (London: St. Anselm's Society, 1910). This 2002 edition by Sophia Institute Press includes minor editorial revisions to the original text and presents the chapters in a different order from that of the original edition.

Sophia Institute Press
Box 5284, Manchester, NH 03108
1-800-888-9344
www.SophiaInstitute.com
Sophia Institute Press® is a registered trademark of Sophia Institute.

Imprimatur: Herbert, Archbishop of Westminster
November 29, 1892

Library of Congress Cataloging-in-Publication Data

Grou, Jean Nicolas, 1731-
    The spiritual life : a comprehensive manual for Catholics seeking salvation / Jean Nicolas Grou.
        p. cm.
    ISBN 1-928832-46-6 (pbk. : alk. paper)
    1. Spiritual life — Catholic Church. I. Dion, Philip E., 1910- Basic spiritual means. II. Title.

BX2350.2.D545 2001
248.4'82 — dc21

                            2001049068

∽

Contents

1. Recognize how precious your soul is to God 3

2. Understand what it
   really means to be devout. 11

3. Let Christ be
   your model in the spiritual life. 17

4. Recognize your nothingness 25

5. Strive to know yourself 33

6. Let God Himself enlighten you 41

7. Be on guard against your heart's weakness. 49

8. Strive to perfect yourself
   and to let God perfect you 57

9. Know what God asks of you
   and what you should ask of God. 65

10. Rely completely on God 73

11. Use your time wisely. 81

12. Learn to profit from your faults 89

13. Do not be discouraged by temptations 97

14. Learn how to deal with your temptations 105

15. Trust God in all things. 113

16. Maintain interior peace 121

17. Be faithful to God in little things 129

18. Let your soul rest in God 137

19. Let the crucifix remind you of God's love 143

20. Remember that all things
    work for good for those who love God 151

    Biographical note: Fr. Jean Nicolas Grou 159

O Lord of my soul!
Can I think of the happiness
Thy children enjoy even in this life
without imploring of Thee with all my heart
to call me also into the number of those children
in whom Thou dost find delight —
of those children who are Thy true worshipers,
who depend entirely on Thee, and
who accomplish Thine adorable will
in all things?

Suffer me, O my Savior,
to come to Thee in like manner!
Take me in Thy sacred arms,
lay Thy hands on me, and bless me.

Take away from me forever
my own spirit,
and replace it by the instinct
of Thy divine grace.
Take from me my own will,
and leave me only the desire of doing Thy will.

Give me that beautiful, that lovable,
that sublime simplicity which is
the first and the greatest of Thy gifts.

Adam was created in this simplicity.
He lost it for himself and for me by his sin.
I have deserved myself, by my innumerable faults,
to be deprived of it forever.

But, my Lord and my God,
O Supreme Good, and my Rest,
Thou canst give it to me again.
Thou dost desire to do so,
and if I put no obstacle in Thy way,
I hope that Thou wilt restore it to me.

Then Thou shalt receive from me
that tribute of homage
which is perfect only from
the mouths of children. Amen.

∞

The Spiritual Life

∞

Chapter One

Recognize how precious your soul is to God

If, on the one hand, religion humbles a man by teaching him that he comes from nothing, that he was conceived in sin, that he is inclined to evil and incapable of any supernatural good, on the other hand, it raises him up and inspires him with great thoughts about himself, by teaching him what his nature is really capable of through the grace of God, what is the greatness of his destiny, and what it cost God to purchase his salvation.

The human soul, by its very nature, is endowed with the faculty of knowing God and the capacity for loving Him. The intelligence of the soul, transporting itself above all that is created and finite, has power to raise itself even to the contemplation of that Being who alone is uncreated and infinite, who is the source of all good and all perfection; it is able to form of Him an idea that is clear and accurate and indelible. The will of the soul is made to love this sovereign Good, which the understanding presents to it. The desires of the soul, which no created object can ever satisfy and which reach far beyond the limits of this life, tend necessarily toward a Good that is supreme, eternal, and infinite, and which alone can content the soul and make it happy.

If the soul will analyze the desire it has of happiness, and the idea of happiness that presents itself to it, it will find that the object of this idea and of this desire is only and can only be God. This is the impression that the soul bears in the depths of its nature; this is what reason will teach it if it will only reflect a little, and this is what neither prejudice nor passion can ever entirely efface. Everything that is not God, everything that does not relate to God, is unworthy of occupying the mind or the heart of man, has no proportion with the immensity of his ideas and desires, and can never fully satisfy them. The very heathen philosophers comprehended this truth up to a certain point, and this was what rendered man so great in their eyes. Happy would they have been if in their conduct they had followed the light of their reason and the secret instinct of their hearts!

Not only is man destined to know and to love God in this life, but in another life he is to possess God eternally. It is not enough for him to be immortal; he is one day to be united to the Source of immortality and to be happy with the very happiness of God. Of what use, indeed, would immortality be to him, if he were to be forever consumed with a desire for God without ever possessing Him? Such a desire, if it were never satisfied, would be only a torment.

This is, then, the final end of man: the eternal enjoyment of God! He will see God; he will contemplate God in Himself, and this sight and this contemplation will overwhelm him with an ineffable joy. Reason puts us in the way of learning this great truth, but Divine Revelation alone can give us distinct instructions on it. And as it is a wonderful gift, which certainly is not due to our nature, we would never have known of it unless God Himself had expressly revealed it. Therefore, there is nothing like it in the writings of the wise men of antiquity.

∞

We must make good use of our free will

But this eternal possession of God is not promised to man absolutely and without conditions; he must merit it by the good use he makes of his free will during this short life. And God, on His part, gives him and offers him everything that is necessary for making a good use of his free will.

And in what does this good use consist? In loving and serving God according to the knowledge with which reason and religion supply him in practicing a certain number of precepts that in themselves contain nothing but what is just and right. Reason cannot help approving of these precepts, and the upright heart is drawn to them. Even in this world, man finds peace and happiness in the observance of these precepts.

How great is man when we consider him from this point of view! How noble are his ideas, how elevated his sentiments, how pure his actions, how worthy he is of the esteem of God and of his fellowmen, when he thinks and speaks and acts always with a view to this sublime destiny, when he never loses sight of it, and when he never allows himself anything that could draw him away from it! What more just and excellent use can he make of his reason and his liberty?

But how small is he, how mean, how foolish, how unjust and cruel to himself, if, confining his ideas and affections to this life, which is passing away, to this life, of which not one single moment is in his own power, he lowers himself to the enjoyment of things that were not made for him, to things that will always leave him empty and craving for more; and if, to procure himself this enjoyment, he tramples underfoot the law of God and exposes himself to the danger of losing forever the eternal happiness that is awaiting him!

Is there any folly to compare with such folly as this? Can the degradation of our being be carried farther? Can a man be a greater enemy to himself? "Be astonished, O heavens," God Himself exclaims at the sight of such a strange perversity. "Gates of Heaven, give yourselves up to desolation! My people" — that is to say, those men that I formed in my own image, whom I destined to be the citizens of my kingdom, to share my glory and felicity — "my people have committed two evils: they have forsaken me, the Fountain of living water [of true happiness], and they have hewed themselves out broken cisterns that can hold no water."[1]

These two evils, which we could hardly believe possible on the part of a reasonable being, are nevertheless two very common evils, very prevalent, and, we might almost say, universal. In every country, in the very midst of enlightenment and religion, nearly all men forget God, despise God, offend God, look upon Him almost as a mortal enemy. And why? Because He created them for Himself, because He has destined them to

[1] Jer. 2:12-13.

enjoy His own happiness, because He wishes to associate them with His own eternal felicity, and because, for this reason, He forbids them to fix their affections on fleeting and perishable pleasures, which are unworthy of them and incapable of ever satisfying them. Almost all men fix their eyes on this earth, which is only the place of their exile, and will not look toward Heaven, which is their true country. They desire immortality only so that they may always possess the goods of this world; and they console themselves for the frightful prospect of death by the hope of returning to the nothingness from which they came.

∞

Remember that our salvation was bought at a great price

But that which puts the crown on the real greatness of man, and on the sad disorder of his abasement of himself, is the thought of what the salvation of his soul has cost God. The Word of God, the eternal Son of God, who was God like His Father and equal in all things to His Father, united Himself to our human nature, took upon Himself our passible and mortal flesh, conversed with men, condescended to instruct them by His teaching and example, and finally, as a voluntary victim, sacrificed Himself for them to the Divine Justice, to expiate their sins, to reconcile them to God, to restore to them the grace of their first innocence from which they had fallen, and to grant them all the assistance and all the means necessary for their salvation. That which our Lord and Savior Jesus Christ did and suffered for all men, He did and suffered for each one in particular; and He would not have thought it too much to do if it had been a question of saving only a single soul. The salvation of a soul is, then, the price of the blood of God, the price of the death of God, the price of the greatest sacrifice that God, clothed in our human nature, could possibly make! This is incomprehensible. And if this mystery were not supported by all the weight of the proofs of a Divine Revelation, human reason could never bring itself to believe it.

But if this mystery is of a truth, and a certainty, and a moral evidence that no reasonable mind can deny, what does it prove? It proves that the dignity of a soul is beyond understanding — for God to abase Himself, for God to annihilate Himself, for God to sacrifice Himself, only to save that soul and make it happy forever!

Can we be afraid of deceiving ourselves, when we esteem that which God esteemed so much? And if, so that we may save ourselves, God required of us the same sacrifice to which Jesus Christ willingly submitted Himself, could we say that He required too much?

Again, what does this mystery prove? It proves that a Christian who knows and understands it, and who, to satisfy a miserable earthly passion, consents to the eternal loss of his own soul, renders useless the sufferings, the death, and the sacrifice of God — and this is not saying enough — he turns them to his eternal damnation and makes for himself a hell a thousand times deeper than that from which Jesus Christ died to deliver him.

And what shall we say of those who, because this mystery is so incomprehensible, treat it as a myth and an absurdity? They do not wish that God should have thought them worth so

much. It was not worth the trouble, they say, that God-made-
man should die for them on a Cross. The human soul is too
small a thing for its happiness to cost God so much. To hear
them speak, it seems as if they were taking the part of God,
and regarding His glory; they seem to think that it is an unbearable pride on the part of men to imagine that their souls
could have such a high value. As if a mystery so divine, so
above human reason, so incredible, could ever have been an
invention of human imagination or the fruit of human pride!
Let us leave these impious ones, who vainly try to justify their
impiety.

As for us, who believe humbly and firmly all that God has
revealed to us, let us learn, by the contemplation of God upon
a Cross, what is the value of our souls. Let us not lose our soul;
let us not prostitute it to creatures; and to make sure of our
eternal salvation, which cost so much to the Son of God, let us
beg of Jesus Christ Himself to take charge of it, to lead us in
the right way and guide us always. Such an inestimable treasure runs too great a risk in our own hands. Let us trust it to
God and our Savior. Let us make Him the Master of our liberty, which we may so easily abuse, and the abuse of which
may bring about such terrible consequences. Once abandoned
to the safe and infallible guidance of His grace, we have no
more to fear. He loves us too much, He takes too much interest
in our salvation, ever to lose the price of His blood and His
sufferings.

Chapter Two

∞

Understand what it really means to be devout

The word *devotion,* which is derived from the Latin, answers to that of devotedness — a vowing of ourselves, a consecration of ourselves. A devout person is, then, a person devoted to God, consecrated to God. There is no stronger expression than that of devotion to mark that disposition of the soul of a person who is ready to do everything and to suffer everything for Him to whom he is devoted.

The devotion to creatures (I mean, of course, that which is lawful and allowed by God) has necessarily its limits. The devotion to God has none, and can have none. As soon as the least reserve, the least exception, intrudes there, it is no longer devotion. True and solid devotion is, then, that disposition of the heart by which we are ready to do and to suffer, without exception or reserve, everything that comes from God's good pleasure, everything that is the will of God. And this disposition is the most excellent of all the gifts of the Holy Spirit. We cannot ask for it too often or too earnestly; and we must never flatter ourselves that we have it in its perfection, because it can always go on increasing, either in itself or in its effects.

∞

Devotion is interior and lasting

We see, by this definition, that devotion is something most interior, which has to do with the inmost life of the soul, for it affects that within us which is most spiritual — that is to say, our understanding and our will. Devotion consists, then, neither in reasoning, nor in imagination, nor in anything that is sensible. We are not devout just because we are able to reason well about the things of God, nor because we have grand ideas or fine imaginations about spiritual matters, nor because we are sometimes affected to tears.

Again, devotion is not a thing that passes, that comes and goes, as it were, but it is something habitual, fixed, permanent, which extends over every instant of life and regulates all our conduct.

The principle of devotion is that, with God being the one Source and the one Author of holiness, the reasonable creature ought to depend on Him in everything and be absolutely governed by the Spirit of God. He must be always attached to God in the depths of his soul, always attentive to His voice within him, always faithful to accomplish what He asks of him each moment.

It is, then, impossible to be truly devout unless we are interior, given to recollection, accustomed to retire within ourselves, or rather never to go out of ourselves, to possess our soul in peace.

Understand what it really means to be devout

Whoever gives himself up to his senses, to his imagination, to his passions, I do not say in criminal things, but even in those which are not bad in themselves, will never be devout; for the first effect of devotion is to bring into captivity the senses, the imagination, and the passions, and to prevent the will from ever being led away by them.

He who is curious, impulsive, delighting to interest himself in exterior things, and to mix himself up with the affairs of others; he who is never willingly alone; he who is critical, speaking ill of his neighbor, sarcastic, irritable, contemptuous, haughty, ready to take offense at anything that wounds his self-love; he who is obstinate, believing only in his own opinions, or he who is a slave to human respect and to public opinion to such an extent that he is in consequence weak, inconstant, and always changing his principles and his conduct will never be devout in the sense I mean.

∞

The devout person seeks God, not himself

The truly devout man is a man of prayer, whose sole delight is to be with God, and to speak with Him, and who scarcely ever loses his sense of the presence of God. Not that he is always thinking of God — for that is impossible here below — but because he is always united to God in his heart and is guided in everything by His Spirit. To pray, he has no need of a book, or of a method, or of great efforts of the head or even of the will. He has only to retire quietly into himself. There he finds God; there he finds peace — sometimes a peace full of joy, sometimes a peace in spite of dryness, but always a deep and real peace. He prefers the prayer in which he gives much to God, and in which he suffers — the prayer in which self-love is undermined gradually, until it can find nothing to feed upon; in short, a simple prayer, denuded of all images or of perceptible feelings and of all those things which the soul can experience in other kinds of prayer.

The truly devout man seeks not himself or his own gratification in the service of God, and he endeavors to practice this maxim of the *Imitation of Christ:* Wherever you find self, renounce self.

The truly devout man studies to fulfill perfectly all the duties of his state and all his really necessary duties of kindness and courtesy to society. He is faithful to his devotional exercises, but he is not a slave to them; he interrupts them, he suspends them, he even gives them up altogether for a time when any reason of necessity or of simple charity requires it. Provided he does not do his own will, he is always certain of doing the will of God.

∞

Devotion calls for simplicity, confidence, and generosity

The truly devout man does not run about seeking for good works, but he waits until the occasion of doing good presents itself to him. He does what in him lies to ensure success; but he leaves the care of the success to God. He prefers those good works which are obscure and done in secret to those which are brilliant and gain general admiration; but he does not shrink from these latter ones when they are for the glory of God and the edification of his neighbor. The truly devout man does not burden himself with a great quantity of vocal prayers and practices that do not leave him time to breathe. He always preserves his liberty of spirit; he is neither scrupulous nor uneasy about himself; he goes on with simplicity and confidence.

He has made a determination, once and for all, to refuse nothing to God, to grant nothing to self-love, and never to commit a voluntary fault; but he does not perplex himself. He goes on courageously; he is not too particular. If he falls into a fault, he does not agitate himself; he humbles himself at the sight of his own weakness; he raises himself up and thinks no more about it.

He is not astonished at his weaknesses, at his falls or his imperfections; he is never discouraged. He knows that he can do nothing, but that God can do everything. He does not rely on his own good thoughts and resolutions, but simply on the grace and the goodness of God. If he were to fall a hundred times a day, he would not despair, but he would stretch out his hands lovingly to God and beg of Him to lift him up and to take pity on him.

The truly devout man has a horror of evil, but he has a still greater love of good. He thinks more about practicing virtue than about avoiding vice. He is generous, large-hearted, and courageous; and when there is a question of exposing himself to danger for God's sake, he does not fear wounds. In a word, he loves better to do what is good, even at the risk of falling into some imperfection, than to omit it through fear of the danger of sinning.

No one is so amiable in the ordinary course of life as a really devout man. He is simple, straightforward, open as the day, unpretentious, gentle, solid, and true; his conversation is pleasing and interesting; he can enter into all innocent amusements; and he carries his condescending kindness and charity as far as possible, short of what is wrong. Whatever some persons may say, true devotion is never a melancholy thing, either for itself or for others. How could the man who continually enjoys the truest happiness — the only happiness — ever be sad? It is the inordinate passions of human nature that are sad — avarice, ambition, love that is not sanctified by God and has not God for its chief end. And it is to divert themselves from the trouble and uneasiness that these passions cause the heart that men plunge themselves recklessly into pleasures and excesses, which they vary continually, but which weary the soul, without ever satisfying it.

Whoever really and in sincerity gives himself up to the service of God will experience the truth of that sentence "To serve God is to reign," even if it be in poverty, in humiliations, and in suffering. All those who in this world seek their happiness in something that is not God — all, without exception — will verify the saying of St. Augustine: The heart of man is made for God alone and is never at peace until it rests in God. "Thou hast made us for Thyself, and our heart findeth no rest until it reposeth in Thee."[2]

---

[2] St. Augustine (354-430; Bishop of Hippo), *Confessions*, Bk. 1, ch. 1.

Chapter Three

∾

Let Christ be your model
in the spiritual life

There are very few Christians, even among those who are especially consecrated to God, who have a right idea of what true virtue is. Almost all of them imagine it to consist in a certain routine of piety and in fidelity to certain exterior practices. If with this they have at intervals some emotion of sensible devotion, without taking care to discern whether these emotions come from God or from their own efforts, they at once conclude that they are really virtuous.

Nevertheless, they are subject to a thousand faults and imperfections, of which they take no heed themselves and which anyone else would try in vain to make them conscious of. They are narrow-minded, scrupulously exact in their practices of devotion, full of esteem for themselves, extremely sensitive and touchy, obstinate in holding their own opinions, puffed up with self-love, constrained and affected in their manners; there is nothing true, nothing simple, nothing natural about them. In their own hearts, they prefer themselves to all others, and often they despise, condemn, and persecute really holy persons and true piety, of which they know nothing.

Nothing is more common in Christianity than this false and pharisaical virtue. Those who are really good have no greater enemies than those who are pharisaical; and if we wish to describe them in a few words, we may say it was persons only pretending to be holy who crucified Jesus Christ, and they still crucify Him every day in His most perfect imitators. As soon as anyone really gives himself to God and begins to lead an inner life, he is sure to draw upon himself, first of all jealousy and criticism, and then persecutions and calumnies of every kind, from these devout Pharisees.

If we wish to understand what true virtue is, we must contemplate it in our Lord and Savior Jesus Christ. He is our one great example; He gave Himself to us for that reason; He was made man so that holiness might be sensible and palpable to us. All sanctity that is not formed and modeled on His sanctity is false. It is displeasing to God. It may perhaps deceive men, but it is useless for Heaven.

Let us, then, make Jesus Christ our study; and so that we may know Him thoroughly, and express His life in ourselves, let us continually ask Him for light and grace.

∞

Jesus sought only God's glory

Jesus Christ sought Himself in nothing; never had He in view His own interests, either temporal or spiritual; never did He perform a single action for the sake of pleasing men, nor did He ever abstain from any good action for fear of displeasing them. God alone — God's glory and His will — was the sole object of His thoughts and feelings, the sole rule of His conduct. He sacrificed all, without reserve, to the interests of His Father.

∞

Jesus' piety was interior

Jesus Christ made piety to consist in our interior dispositions, the religion of the heart; not in vain, fleeting feelings, but in sincere and efficacious resolutions, always followed by execution; a disposition of an entire devotion to God, a continual annihilation of self, and a boundless charity toward others.

Every instant of His life was consecrated to the accomplishment of these three dispositions. He neglected no observance of any point of the law; but, at the same time, He declared, both by word and example, that this observance was only of value when it proceeded from an inner principle of love, and that the practice of the letter of the law alone, without the interior spirit, made slaves, and not children of God.

∞

Jesus strove for the eternal, not the temporal

Jesus Christ always looked upon this present life as passing away; as a pilgrimage, a time of trial, simply designed to test our love for God. The things that are eternal were His constant occupation. He gave to nature what was absolutely necessary, without going beyond. Although He possessed nothing and was always dependent on Providence for His simple bodily wants, He was never uneasy about the morrow, and His delight was to experience the effects of poverty.

Jesus Christ embraced by His own free choice that which men accept with the greatest difficulty and to which they submit only out of necessity. He did not absolutely condemn riches, but He preferred poverty. He did not condemn the rank and marks of honor that God Himself has established among men, but He taught us that an obscure condition, bereft of every kind of consideration, is more pleasing to God and more favorable for salvation; and that to think ourselves better than others because we are born great, noble, or powerful, or are in a position of authority is an error and the source of countless sins. With the exception of the simple natural pleasure that the Creator has attached to certain actions, and the use of which is limited by the severest rules, He has absolutely scorned every other kind of pleasure, especially those which men seek with the greatest eagerness, and, as far as He Himself was concerned, He renounced even the most innocent pleasure. Hard work, apostolic labors, prayer, and the instruction of His disciples and the multitude filled up every moment of His life.

∞

Jesus was a model of simplicity

Jesus Christ was simplicity itself, always the same, without any affectation in His speech or actions. With the authority of God-made-man, He taught the most sublime truths and things that had before been unknown. But He propounded His doctrine in a simple, familiar manner, without any pomp of human eloquence, and so that all minds could understand Him. His miracles, divine in themselves, are still more divine from the way in which He wrought them. He wished that the account of the evangelists should agree with the perfect simplicity of His own life. It is impossible to give in a simpler manner than they have done the account of a life, and of words and actions, that bear on them the very impress of Divinity.

∞

Jesus was merciful

Jesus Christ had a most tender compassion for sinners who were sincerely humble and repentant for their sins. "I came for sinners," He said, "and not for the just," who trust in their own justice.[3] The publican who stood afar off, Mary Magdalene, the woman taken in adultery, and the Samaritan woman at the well of Jacob were all treated by Him with a kindness and tenderness that astonishes us. But the pride of the Pharisees, their hypocrisy, their avarice — these were the objects of His most severe censure and malediction. The sins of the mind and the spirit, the very sins to which the falsely devout are more subject than any others, are those which He condemned with the greatest severity, because they are a sign of more blindness of the mind and more corruption of the heart.

Jesus Christ bore with a never-failing gentleness the faults and the roughness of His disciples. According to our way of thinking, what must He not have suffered at having to live with men so imperfect and so ignorant of the things of God?

---

[3] Cf. Mark 2:17.

The Spiritual Life

Dealing with our neighbor is perhaps one of the most difficult things in this life; even the saints have felt how much it cost them. And the nearer they are to God, the more they need to lower themselves to others, as it were, to unbend, to conceal and excuse in others a thousand faults that they see and feel more keenly than anyone else. And this is a point on which their practice must be continual, and it all depends on how they acquit themselves with regard to it as to whether they will make virtue amiable or displeasing to others.

⚭

Jesus accepted suffering

Jesus Christ suffered every kind of persecution at the hands of His enemies, but He never gave way. He only opposed to them His innocence and virtue, and He always confounded them by His spotless life. When the hour came that He allowed Himself to fall into their hands, He permitted their evil passions to act and looked on them as instruments of divine justice. He kept silence when He saw them so obstinate in their malice. He sought not to justify Himself, although it would have been so easy. He allowed Himself to be condemned. He allowed them to enjoy their imaginary triumph. He pardoned them; He prayed for them; He shed His blood for them. This is the most sublime and the most difficult height of perfection.

Whoever aspires to true sanctity, and to be guided in everything by the Spirit of God, must expect to suffer from the tongues of men, to bear their calumnies and sometimes their persecutions. In this, above all things, we must take Jesus Christ as our model. We must suffer, for His sake, as much as we can, in the interests of truth. Our only answer to calumny must be the innocence of our life; we must keep silence when it is not absolutely necessary to speak. We must leave the care of our justification to God, if He sees fit to justify us. We must stifle in our heart every feeling of resentment and bitterness. We must try to soften our enemies by every kind of charitable actions. We must pray to God for their pardon; and we must try to see, in all they make us suffer only the accomplishment of God's designs upon us.

And when virtue can thus sustain itself in contempt, in opprobrium, in ill treatment, then we may look upon it as perfected, as consummate virtue. Therefore, God generally reserves this trial to the last. Blessed are those who pass through it! When Jesus Christ comes in His glory, they will have a share in it proportionate to their share in His humiliations. To desire such a state as this, to accept it when it is offered to us, to bear it patiently and with joy when we find ourselves in it — this can only be the effect of grace, and of an extraordinary grace. As for us, let us rest content in our lowliness; let us never think we can attain of ourselves to anything so high; and let us only ask of God that human respect may never cause us to abandon His interests.

∞

Chapter Four

Recognize your nothingness

When we are spoken to of dying to ourselves, of annihilating ourselves, when we are told that that is the foundation of Christian morality and that in it consists the adoration of God in spirit and in truth, we do not wish to receive this saying. It seems to us hard and even unjust, and we rebel against those who announce it to us on the part of God. Let us convince ourselves once and for all that this saying has nothing but what is just and right in itself, and that the practice of it is infinitely sweeter than we think. Afterward let us humble ourselves if we have not the courage to put it in practice, and instead of condemning the words of wisdom, let us condemn ourselves.

What does God ask of us, when He commands us to annihilate ourselves and to renounce ourselves? He asks of us to do ourselves justice, to put ourselves in our proper place, and to acknowledge ourselves for what we really are. Even if we had been born and had always lived in a state of innocence, even if we had never lost original grace, we would still be nothing else but utter nothingness from our very nature; we could not look on ourselves otherwise without making a great mistake; and we would be unjust if we expected God or men to look on us in any other light.

What rights can a thing have that is nothing? What can a thing require that is nothing? If his very existence is a free gift, certainly everything else he has is much more so. It is, then, a formal injustice on our part to refuse to be treated, or to refuse to treat ourselves, as if we were really nothing.

But we may say that this avowal costs us nothing to make with regard to God, and that it is just as far as He is concerned, but that it is not at all so with regard to other men, who are nothing as well as we are, and therefore have no right to oblige us to such an avowal and to all its consequences.

Certainly, this avowal costs us nothing as far as God is concerned, if we make it only with our mouth; but if we mold our conduct on it and allow God to exercise over us all the rights that belong to Him; if we freely consent that He shall dispose of us as He pleases, of our mind, our heart, and our whole being, it will cost us a great deal, and we shall even find a difficulty in not saying that it is injustice. Therefore, God has pity on our weakness; He does not make use of His rights in all their severity; and He never puts us to certain annihilating trials without first having obtained our free consent.

∽

Injustices that we suffer
are really injustices against God

As to what concerns men, I agree that of themselves they have no authority over us, and that any contempt or outrage or humiliation on their part is an injustice. But we have no right to complain of this injustice for that reason, because in reality it is not an injustice against us, who are nothing and to whom nothing is due; but it is an injustice against God, whose commands they violate when they despise us, or humble us, or outrage us. It is therefore God who should resent the injury they do to Him by ill-treating us; it is not for us to resent it, for in all that happens to us, we ought to feel only the injury that is done to God.

My neighbor despises me; he is wrong, because he is of no more importance than I am, and God has forbidden him to despise me. But is he wrong because I am really worthy of esteem and because there is nothing in me that deserves contempt? No. If he takes away from me my goods, if he blackens my reputation, if he attempts to take my life, he is guilty, and very guilty, toward God. But is he so toward me? Am I justified in wishing him ill for it, or in seeking revenge? No, because all that I possess, all that I am, is not properly mine, who have nothing of my own but nothingness and from whom, therefore, nothing can be taken away.

If we were always to look upon things thus, only as they regard God's side of the question, and not ours, we would not be so easily wounded, so sensitive, so given to complaining and getting angry. All our disturbances come from thinking ourselves to be something of importance and assuming rights that we do not possess, and because we always, and in all things, begin by considering ourselves directly and do not attend to the rights and interests of God, which alone are offended in our persons.

The Spiritual Life

∞

Injustices from others are less than our sins deserve

I confess that this is a very difficult practice and that, to attain to it, we must be dead to ourselves. But indeed it is a just thing, and reason has nothing to oppose to it. For God requires of us nothing but what is reasonable when He requires of us that we should behave toward Him and toward our neighbor as if we were nothing, had nothing, and expected nothing.

This would be quite just, as I have already said, even if we had preserved our first innocence. But because we were born in Original Sin, and if we have stained ourselves over and over with actual sins, if we have contracted innumerable debts against divine justice, if we have deserved, I know not how many times, eternal damnation — is it not a chastisement far too mild for us to be treated as if we were nothing, and is not a sinner infinitely beneath that which is nothing? Whatever trial he may suffer from God, whatever ill treatment he may have to bear from his neighbor, has he any right to complain? Can he accuse God of severity, or men of injustice? Ought he not to think himself too happy to be able to save himself from eternal torments by patiently bearing these small temporal trials?

If religion is not a delusion altogether, if what Faith teaches us about sin and the punishments it incurs is really true, how can a sinner whom God wishes to pardon dare to think that he does not deserve whatever he may have to endure here below, even if his life were to last for millions of ages?

Yes, it is a sovereign injustice, it is a monstrous ingratitude, for anyone who has offended God — and which of us has not offended Him? — not to accept with a good heart and most thankfully, with love and zeal for the interests of God, all that it may please the Divine Goodness to send him in the way of sufferings and humiliations.

And what shall we say if these sufferings, these passing humiliations, are not merely to be instead of the punishments of Hell, but if they are to be the price of an eternal felicity, of the eternal possession of God — if we are to be raised high in glory in proportion as we have been humbled and annihilated in this world? Shall we still fear this annihilation? And shall we think that we are being wronged when we are required to annihilate ourselves because we are really nothing, and because we are sinners while all the time we have the promise of a reward that will never end?

∾

Dying to ourselves will bring us peace

I may add that this way of annihilation, against which nature cries out so strongly, is not really so painful as we imagine, and it is even sweet. For first, our Lord and Savior, Jesus Christ has said so. "Take my yoke upon you," He says, "for it is easy and light."[4] However heavy this yoke may be in itself, God will lighten it for those who willingly take it up and consent to bear it for the love of Him. Love does not prevent us from suffering, but it makes us love our sufferings and prefer them to all pleasures.

The reward, even in this world, of annihilating ourselves, is peace of heart — a calming of our passions, a cessation of all

[4] Cf. Matt. 11:29-30.

the agitations of our mind and of all murmurs and interior revolts.

Let us examine the proof of this in detail. What is the greatest evil of suffering? It is not the suffering itself, but our rebellion against it. It is the state of interior revolt that so often accompanies it. A soul that is perfectly annihilated will suffer all the evils imaginable without losing the sweet repose of its blessed state: this is a matter of experience.

It costs a great deal to attain this state of annihilation; we must make the greatest efforts over ourselves. But when we have attained it, we enjoy a peace and repose proportionate to the victories we have gained. The habit of renouncing ourselves and of dying to ourselves becomes every day easier and easier, and we are astonished at last to find that what seemed to us once intolerable, what so frightened our imaginations, raised our passions, and put our whole nature in a state of rebellion does not give us even the least pain after a certain time.

In all contempt we may have to suffer, in all calumnies and humiliations, the thing that really hurts us and really makes them hard to bear is our own pride. It is because we wish to be esteemed and considered and treated with a certain respect, and that we do not at all like the idea of being treated with ridicule and contempt by others. This is what really agitates us, and makes us indignant, and renders our life bitter and insupportable.

Let us set seriously to work to annihilate ourselves. Let us give no food to pride. Let us put away from us all the first movements of self-esteem and self-love, and let us accept patiently and joyfully, in the depth of our soul, all the little mortifications that are offered to us. Little by little, we shall come not to care in the very least about what is thought of us or said of us, or how we are treated. A person who is dead feels nothing; for him there is no more honor or reputation; praise and blame to him are equal.

In the service of God, the cause of most of the trouble we experience is that we do not annihilate ourselves sufficiently in His divine presence. It is because we have a sort of life that we try to preserve in all our dealings with Him. It is because we allow a secret pride to insinuate itself into our devotion. Hence it comes that we are not indifferent as we ought to be, as to whether we are in dryness or in consolation; that we are very unhappy when God seems to withdraw from us; that we exhaust ourselves in desires and efforts to call Him back to us and fall into the most wretched depression and desolation if His absence lasts a long time.

From this cause, too, proceeds all our false alarms about the state of our souls. We think God must be angry with us because He deprives us of the sweetness of sensible devotion. We think our Communions have been bad because we have made them without relish; the same with our spiritual reading, our prayer, and all our other practices of piety.

Let us serve God, once and for all, in the spirit of annihilation. Let us serve Him for Him alone, not for ourselves. Let us sacrifice our own interests for His glory and His good pleasure. Then we shall always be quite content with the way He treats us, being persuaded that we deserve nothing and that He is too good, I do not say to accept, but to permit, our services.

The Spiritual Life

In all great temptations against purity, or against faith or hope, what is most painful to us is not exactly our fear of offending God, but our fear of losing ourselves through offending Him. We are much more occupied with the thought of our own interest than of His glory. This is why our confessor has so much difficulty in reassuring us and in making us obey him. We think he is deceiving us, that he is leading us astray, that he is ruining us, because he requires us to pass over and set aside our vain fears.

Let us annihilate our own judgment. Let us prefer blind obedience to all else. Let us even consent, if necessary, to be lost through obedience. Then we shall find that all our perplexities, all the anguish of our soul, all our interior torments will cease. We shall find peace, and a most exquisite and perfect peace, in the total forgetfulness of ourselves. There is nothing in Heaven or on earth or in Hell that can trouble the peace of a soul that is really annihilated.

Chapter Five

Strive to know yourself

"The heart is perverse above all things, and unsearchable: who can know it?"[5] By these words — *the human heart* — we mean that depth of malignity, of perversity, and of self-love that is in every one of us, and whose venom extends over all our actions — even the best of them. For there is scarcely any action we do that is not stained by self-love and deprived of some of its goodness.

This perverse and corrupt element in our nature is a consequence of Original Sin, which has led astray the primitive uprightness of our hearts and has concentrated on our own selves that affection that ought to be given to God alone. If we observe ourselves carefully, we shall find that we love everything in proportion as it affects ourselves, that we judge everything according to our own view of it and solely with regard to our own interests. Instead of this, we ought to love everything, and even ourselves, only in God and for God's sake, and we should judge everything according to the judgment of God

[5] Jer. 17:9.

and in conformity with His interests. And the source of all our vices — those of the mind and those of the heart — is that we reverse this right order of things. This is the root of all our sins and the sole cause of our eternal ruin.

If we study young children, we shall perceive in them the first seeds of this disorder and the germs of all the evil passions of our nature. These germs develop from day to day and have already made serious progress before reason and religion can do anything to check them. And the saddest thing about the whole matter is that the first effect of this disorder is to blind us as to our own state. We can see the faults of others plainly enough, but we cannot and will not see our own; we are angry with those who try to make us see ourselves as we really are, and we will never allow that they are right.

And the principal cause of our trouble when we do fall into a fault is a secret pride that makes us vexed and irritated at be-ing obliged to acknowledge our fall even to ourselves. We do all we possibly can to hide what we really are from ourselves and from others. We do not always succeed with others, who easily find us out; but, unfortunately, we succeed only too well with ourselves.

And the knowledge of our own hearts, which is the most necessary of all knowledge, is also the most rare and that which we take the least trouble to obtain. We live and die without really knowing ourselves, without doing anything to acquire that knowledge, and almost always after having la-bored all our lives to disguise ourselves in our own eyes.

What a terrible mistake, when we have to appear at last be-fore the God of truth, there at last to see ourselves as we really are! Then it will be too late; then there will be no help and no hope. We shall know ourselves but for our own misery and our eternal despair!

It is necessary, therefore, to try in this life to attain to a right knowledge of ourselves and to judge ourselves with a just judgment. And above all, we must try to be firmly persuaded not only of the importance, but of the absolute necessity, of this self-knowledge and also of its extreme difficulty.

But how shall we set about this, when from our earliest childhood we are so profoundly in the dark on this subject, and when increasing age only increases the darkness and obscurity?

∞

Ask God to help you know yourself

We must have recourse to Him who alone knows us perfectly, who has fathomed the most secret recesses of our hearts, who has counted and followed all our footsteps. We must implore the light of His grace, and by the help of that light we must incessantly study all our actions and the secret motives of those actions — all our inclinations, our affections, our passions; above all, those which seem the most refined and the most spiritual. We must be inexorable in condemning ourselves whenever we see we are guilty and never try to excuse ourselves either in the sight of others or in our own sight.

If we are in this good disposition of uprightness and sincerity, if we acknowledge humbly before God our own blindness with regard to ourselves, most assuredly He will enlighten us; and if we will only make good use of these first rays of His divine light, we shall see more and more clearly, day by day, into our own hearts. We shall discover by degrees all our defects, even those that were most imperceptible; even the cunning deceits of self-love will not be able to escape from our vision. And, aided by the divine assistance, we shall pursue this enemy relentlessly until we succeed in banishing him forever from our hearts.

Now, God, who is infinitely wise, gives us this knowledge of ourselves only gradually and by degrees. He does not show us our misery all at once; such a sight would drive us to despair, and we would not have strength to bear it. But He shows us first of all our most glaring faults; and as we go on correcting these, He reveals to us our more subtle and secret faults, until at last He lays bare to us all the innermost recesses of our hearts.

And this goes on our whole life long; and too happy shall we be if before our death we attain to a perfect knowledge of ourselves and an entire cure of all our evils! This grace is granted only to those souls who are most holy, most faithful, and most generous in never forgiving themselves anything.

∞

God's guidance will keep us from falling
The most important point is, therefore, always to walk under the guidance of the divine light; to be quite sure that, if we wander away from that light, we shall lose ourselves; to mistrust our own intellect, our own judgment, our own opinions, and to be guided in everything by the Spirit of God; to wait for His decision and to hold our own in suspense until He decides

for us and directs us. How rare is such a practice as this, and what great fidelity in mortifying ourselves it requires! But also, by it, what errors we avoid, what falls we escape, what progress we make in perfection!

What errors we avoid! It is certain that whenever we judge the things of God by our own judgment, we are at fault; that we deceive ourselves in everything respecting the nature of holiness and the means of attaining it; that we are as incapable of judging our own actions, motives, and dispositions as we are of judging the actions and dispositions of our neighbor; that in him as in ourselves we condemn where we ought to approve, and approve where we ought to condemn, on slight grounds and without any knowledge of the true state of the case. And as our judgments on such matters are the principles of our conduct, into what errors we fall when we take the promptings of our own spirit for our guide! We construct our own ideal of sanctity; we are quite delighted with it and adhere to it most obstinately; we will listen to no one else's ideas; we judge ourselves and we judge others by this rule, and we thus make terrible mistakes of which everyone but us is conscious!

What falls we escape! All our faults come from leaving the Spirit of God to follow our own spirit. We are not sufficiently careful about this in the beginning. We do not mistrust ourselves enough. We do not always consult God with the deepest humility. We lean on our own spirit until insensibly it takes the place of the Spirit of God. We do not perceive this; at last we deceive ourselves completely and fall into all sorts of delusions. We think we are following the divine light, and we are following only our own imagination, our own passions.

This blindness goes on increasing day by day; the wisest advice cannot bring us back; we are no longer in a state even to listen to it; and — I am not afraid to say it — with the best and most upright intentions in the world, we find ourselves incessantly in danger of committing the greatest faults unless we are really interior and unless we are always on the watch against the artifices of self-love.

There is only one way of making a real advance in the way of perfection, and that is never to guide ourselves, but always to take God for our guide, to renounce ourselves in all things, to die in all things to our own judgment and to our own will. Whatever progress we may have made in this way, the moment we attempt to guide ourselves, we go back. The farther we advance, the more absolutely necessary is the divine guidance for us; and if the greatest saint on earth were to think for a single instant that he could guide himself, in that instant he would be in the greatest danger of being lost forever.

Since, then, it is quite impossible for us to know our own heart, since self-love can always lead us astray and blind us, since pride, which is the greatest of all sins, is all the more to be feared the farther we are advanced in the ways of God, let us never rely on ourselves. Let us always keep ourselves in God's sight and under the guidance of His hand, and let us beg Him to enlighten us always and without ceasing.

The true knowledge of ourselves consists in believing that, however far advanced in perfection we may be, we are always of ourselves incapable in this supernatural life of one good thought, of one right judgment, or of one just action; and that, on the contrary, we are capable of falling into the greatest sins, and even of being hopelessly lost, if we turn away from God and His guidance ever so little. Whoever knows himself in this manner, and acts accordingly, will never go astray. But to know ourselves like this, and to act on our knowledge, we must be really interior, given to recollection, to prayer, and the constant thought of the presence of God.

Chapter Six

∞

Let God Himself enlighten you

Our Lord Jesus Christ said, "For judgment I am come into this world; that they who see might not see, and that they who see might be made blind."[6] Our Savior uttered these words with relation to the man who was born blind and to whom He granted sight of the soul, after having restored to him the sight of the body, in the presence of the Pharisees, whom this miracle ought to have enlightened, and who were only made blinder than ever by it.

The hidden meaning of this sentence of our Lord and Savior Jesus Christ is very deep and is meant for us all. Let us try to penetrate it, by the help of His grace.

∞

Remember that we are all spiritually blind

We are all born blind as a deplorable consequence of Original Sin. We know neither God nor ourselves. We are in profound ignorance as to our destination; that it to say, as to the

---

[6] John 9:39.

one thing that is indisputably the most important of all, or rather, the one thing that alone is truly interesting to us. We neither know in what true happiness consists, nor what steps we must take to attain it.

This ignorance is a fact to which the whole universe bears witness. We have only to remember what was the state of the world before the coming of Jesus Christ, and what is still the state of the nations to whom He is unknown. But this ignorance is not the greatest evil. We are blind, and we do not know that we are blind. Born with this disease, we think ourselves in perfect health; and we would never have known anything about our blindness if God-made-man had not come to deliver us from it.

The greatest of all evils is to think that we see when we do not see. This was the evil of the feigned wise men of paganism and of the proud Pharisees of Judaism.

Now, although Christianity has enlightened us in some degree on essential matters, it has not entirely done away with our blindness. As long as our trust in our own spirit, as long as our self-love, reigns in us, we are blind in many respects, as regards both God and ourselves. As regards God: we understand nothing of His ways; we entertain quite false ideas as to holiness; we know not in what true virtue consists. As regards ourselves: the real mainspring of our dispositions is unknown to us; we can see the faults of others clearly enough, but our own faults are hidden from us; our judgment, in all that regards ourselves, is nothing but a delusion. And as this blindness affects the soul, the soul is not conscious of it, and cannot be; for how can it see by its own light that which it sees not?

Let God Himself enlighten you

∞

Jesus enlightens those who acknowledge their blindness

This evil is very great, but it is not without remedy; it is not hopeless. The divine light can disperse this blindness easily, when it is not voluntary.

But how can the divine light disperse a blindness that we will not acknowledge? How can it enlighten those proud souls who think they see everything and who reject the light because they imagine they have no need of it? What means can it take to penetrate those perverse spirits, led away by a thousand prejudices, obstinate in not seeing what it tries to show them, and determined to see things only in a false light they have created for themselves? This is a very common disease with pious persons; and because the root of it is pride, it opposes to divine grace an obstacle that only humility can overcome, but does not always overcome.

Jesus Christ is the Light of the world; He came to cure our blindness. But in doing this, He exercises a kind of judgment that is full of goodness for some and of justice for others. He gives sight to those who see not, and He blinds those who see. What do these words mean? Do they mean that, among men, before our Lord enlightens them, there are some who see and others who do not see? No, all are equally blind. But some, enlightened by grace as to their sad state, acknowledge humbly that they are blind; they implore our Lord earnestly and with importunity for their cure. To them He will give sight, and He will never cease to grant them that sight as long as they make a good use of the light He has granted them and allow themselves to be entirely guided by it. Others will not confess that they are blind, and these He will leave in their blindness, until it becomes incurable. Either they attribute to themselves the light they receive from Him, and appropriate it as if it came from themselves, and so, as a punishment, He takes it away from them; or they make a bad use of the light He gives them; they neglect its warnings; they fear it and fly from it; and so most justly do they deserve that He should deprive them of it.

Now, to which of these classes do we belong, and do we wish to belong? Unhappy shall we be if we cleave to the lead-ings of our own self-will, if we use our own judgment with re-gard to the ways of God and act in all things as our own spirit prompts us! God will leave us to ourselves! And what can hap-pen to a blind man who attempts to guide himself, but to fall over a precipice?

Unhappy also shall we be if we regard as our own the light that God sends us, if we look on it as our own property, if we are vain of it, if we make use of it only to nourish our pride and presumption! The jealousy of God will never pardon us such a theft. He will take away that light from us. He will never suffer us to usurp His gifts.

And finally, unhappy shall we be if we do not draw from the light we receive all the profit that God intends us to draw from it, if we fear to be enlightened as to what He asks of us, because we cannot make up our minds to grant Him all! He will give to others the light He intended for us; and instead of advancing in the way of perfection, we shall fall back.

Let us, then, imitate the poor blind man in the Gospel; let us be fully convinced that we are always enveloped in darkness and that of ourselves we have no power to free ourselves from it. Let us say continually to Jesus Christ, "Lord, that I may see!"[7] Give me light, either by Thine own voice in my soul, or by the voice of him whom Thou dost wish to be my guide.

If we have to consider anything, let us fear to decide of ourselves; let us fear to act through a natural instinct, through a movement of passion, through prejudice, or human respect; but let us humbly ask of God that He will enlighten us, that He will show us the truth and give us the strength and courage to follow it. Let us keep our soul in a state of continual dependence on the divine light, and let us feel convinced that if God's light leaves us for a single instant, we shall make a false step.

Let us give thanks to God for all the light He gives us, acknowledging that it is from Him alone that we receive it. Let us never rely on our own judgment or on the penetration of our own mind. The things of God can be understood only by the spirit of God. He takes pleasure in enlightening simple souls, who are convinced of their own ignorance and who attribute nothing to themselves; who judge nothing by their own judgment and who give to God the sole glory of all they know and experience, recognizing Him as the Source of all good.

∞

Do not be led by your own spirit

Oh, if we could know how dangerous it is to follow the leading of our own spirit, how much God wishes to humble it,

[7] Luke 18:41.

to cast it down, to annihilate it, we would never rest until we had trampled it underfoot. We would sacrifice it with the greatest joy; we would think ourselves happy if we could foresee nothing, reflect on nothing, not say a single word, nor have a single thought, nor form a single judgment of ourselves, but in all these things depend entirely on the divine guidance. We would endeavor always to keep in our souls a sort of empty space, as it were, for God to fill it as He pleases, and we would carefully suppress every thought that we feel to be our own!

Happy is that state of prayer, happy is the entire state of that soul in which the human spirit acts no longer; it is a proof that God has taken entire possession of it and that He wishes to be the sole Master there. Let us not complain if this state is somewhat painful to human nature. It may be a kind of blindness, but it is a blindness that is produced by the very splendor of the divine light. We may not be able to see anything distinctly, but by virtue of that same light, when it is necessary and God wishes us to see, we shall see well enough; we shall know what we have to do. And what can we need more? Is not the repose of our spirit in God far preferable to any exercise of it independent of God?

Finally, let us make use of the light that God gives us, either to discover our own misery, and so humble us, or to discern what God wishes us to do and practice it, or to show us our faults and help us to correct them. Let us not be afraid of the sight God gives us, because it shows us what perhaps we would rather not see, or nerves us to do what our cowardice shrinks from. Let us not hate the mirror that shows us our own ugliness; let us love the truth that reproves us; and let us believe that after the knowledge of God there is nothing so useful for us as the true knowledge of ourselves. More than this, let us be persuaded that we shall be raised to the true knowledge of God only in proportion as we know and feel our own nothingness. These are the two abysses which "call to each other" according to the expression of Holy Scripture.[8] And blind as we are with regard to these two things, which nevertheless comprise everything for us, let us say with St. Augustine, "Let me know Thee, Lord, and let me know myself."

[8] Cf. Ps. 41:8 (RSV = Ps. 42:7).

Chapter Seven

༄

Be on guard against your heart's weakness

We have been considering how blind is the natural understanding of man; and now we will see also how his heart is naturally weak and corrupted. When I say *weak,* I mean when there is a question of doing good; his heart is only too strong when there is a question of doing evil.

This will of man, which God created upright and pure, has been corrupted by Original Sin, and we are all born in this unfortunate and hereditary corruption. The order of creation has been reversed. Once the heart of man had a natural inclination to love God above all things. But since sin entered into the world, all our love is bestowed on ourselves, and we love nothing but as it affects ourselves. Again, if this love of ourselves was reasonable, if we really understood our true interests, this very love would lead us quickly to God, our First Beginning and our Last End. But it is not reason, it is not our true interests, that regulate our self-love. This love is unreasonable, because it makes us our own end and our own center:

it is contrary to our true interests, because it looks only to a present and temporary good, to a sensible advantage, and entirely loses sight of a divine and spiritual good, of supernatural and eternal advantages.

Hence it happens that from our earliest childhood we seek after earthly things with the whole strength of our souls; that we look for happiness only in the enjoyment of them; that the necessities and pleasures of our body occupy and enslave us; and that our soul, buried, so to speak, in matter and material things, either cannot rise at all, or rises only with the greatest difficulty toward spiritual things.

From this comes that terrible concupiscence, the source of almost all our sins. The saints know this, and groan over it, because they feel how humiliating it is for them, to how many temptations it exposes them, and how contrary it is to the primitive order, which made the soul subject to God, and the body to the soul.

But the greater number of men, and even of Christians, instead of deploring this cruel malady, cherish it, take a pride in themselves for it, and would even think themselves unfortunate if they were not subject to it. For the man without passions seems to them a being without emotion and without life. And the man who fights against his passions, instead of yielding, passes, in their eyes, for a fool and an enemy of his own happiness.

This is the cause of that frightful difficulty we find in practicing Christian morality, the end and aim of which is to destroy in us the reign of concupiscence. And if Christian morality seems to us beautiful, reasonable, and worthy of the dignity of man, we must not think that we so regard it by our natural and human light. Never could it appear so to us if we were not enlightened by the rays of divine grace.

∞

It is difficult to do the good that we know we should do
But how far it is from clearly seeing that the teachings of Christian morality are beautiful to practicing them! By the aid of grace, we form good resolutions; we promise God that we will be faithful to Him; we think ourselves firm and immovable in virtue. But, alas! At the first occasion, the first temptation, we fail; the least difficulty frightens us; the attraction of a sensible and present good makes us forget everything. In a word, we fall at every step; and it is impossible for us to raise ourselves up again by our own strength. What weakness! How humiliating it is!

I do not do the good I wish to do; but the evil I wish not to do, that I do.[9] Again, if I wish to do good, although it may be only a feeble desire, and if I do not wish to do evil, this is all the gift of divine grace; for the corruption and malice of my will are such that its first natural movements would draw it away from good and incline it to evil. We need not watch ourselves for a long time to discover this sad disposition. Our heart is almost always at war with reason. Reason advises us to do such and such a thing; passion advises us the exact contrary. We see, and we approve of, the better part; but we follow the worst. Even pagans have remarked this. This constant

[9] Cf. Rom. 7:15.

fight between reason and the passions keeps the soul in one continual state of agitation.

But this is only the beginning of our malice. Our natural malice is irritated at the forbidding of evil; it is angry with God, who is the Author of this prohibition. It exhausts itself in reasonings, in subtle arguments, to persuade itself that such a prohibition is unjust and tyrannical and that man has a right to give himself up, without restraint and without measure, to the guidance of his passions.

Listen to self-love; self-love wishes to be the master of all; he pretends that everything belongs to him; he has no respect for the rights of others. Any resistance that is opposed to what he desires seems to him an injustice. He envies others for what they have and he has not; not only does he envy them, but he tries by every means to take away from them what they have.

And it is quite certain that passion would stop at nothing, if it were strong enough to tear down the barriers. It is never the fear of God that arrests its fury; it is simply the fear of man and of human laws; therefore, passion will substitute fraud and deception, as much as it can, for violence. And the crime is committed in the heart, even if we are wanting in the courage and the means to carry it out.

Many disorders are committed in the world; but incomparably more are committed in the secret of men's hearts that are never able to be actually committed for want of occasion and resources. Whoever could look secretly upon all that men desire, resolve, and execute in the interior of their mind would find them a thousand times more wicked than they appear outwardly.

Be on guard against your heart's weakness

Not only does the prohibition of evil irritate man; it is actually an additional attraction to make him commit evil. The law, far from arresting the will, only excites it; and the great charm of sin is that it is sin. St. Paul has said it,[10] and daily experience only shows it to us too well: it is quite sufficient for a thing to be forbidden us to make us instantly desire to do it. A book, a picture, or a play has been forbidden to us; at once our curiosity is aroused, and we have no rest until it is satisfied. What has been hidden from us is the thing of all others we desire to know. What has been refused to us is the thing of all others we desire to have. It seems as if every law, every restraint, were an attempt against our liberty; and as if neither God nor man had any right to control our desires. Can the corruption and malice of our will be carried any further?

∽

Beware of glorying in your miseries

The worst of all is that, instead of being covered with confusion at all these miseries, we glory in them. Instead of condemning them, or at least excusing them, we seek to justify them. We boast of the evil we have done and even of that which we have not really done; we advertise ourselves as more wicked than we really are. The great triumph of libertines, when they are together, is to surpass themselves in this manner. And their only shame is when they see that others have succeeded in carrying their wicked pleasures and debaucheries farther than they themselves have.

[10] Cf. Rom. 7:9-13.

The Spiritual Life

If we do not feel ourselves capable of such excesses as these, we know ourselves very imperfectly. The root of corruption is the same in all hearts; nothing is necessary but to give ourselves up freely to any single passion, and at once the corruption is developed.

Let us go a little way into the depths of our own heart; let us recall what has happened there in certain circumstances; let us see where such a desire, such an inclination, such a feeling would have led us if education, fear, and religion had not restrained us, or if the occasion had not been wanting. Let us be just to ourselves; and let us confess in all humility that if God had not specially watched over us, there is no crime, however terrible, into which our natural corruption might not have led us. Let us thank God, both for those sins which He has forgiven us, and for those from which He has preserved us. And let us say, with St. Augustine, that there is no crime that one man has committed that another man is not capable of, and that he would not, perhaps, commit, in very deed, if it were not for the divine assistance.

∞

God gradually reveals our weaknesses to us

The depth of our misery is so great that we could not possibly bear the full sight of it; and if God were to allow us to see it as it is, when we begin to give ourselves to Him, the sight would drive us to despair. Therefore, He shows it to us only by degrees, and with a reserve that is full of wisdom. But as this knowledge of our true selves is absolutely necessary for us to make us humble, watchful, and full of distrust of our own

strength and full of confidence in God, by degrees, and gradually, as we grow stronger and advance in virtue, God will show
us our natural corruption and our weakness. And by the greatness of the evil, He will make us judge the price of the remedy;
He will make us approach that dreadful abyss from which His
grace has drawn us back and will reveal to us all the profound-
ness of its depth. Thus, He made St. Teresa[11] see the very place
in Hell that she would have occupied if He had not called her
to Himself by His infinite mercy. And it is thus that the sins
we have actually committed, and those we might have committed were it not for the assistance of His grace, are made to
serve as a foundation for our humility and our sanctity.

But God does not stop there with those souls He deigns to
call to the highest perfection. He is not contented with giving
to them a speculative knowledge of their misery; He will give
to them an experiential knowledge.

For this He waits until their will is so confirmed and rooted
in good that there is no longer any fear that they will actually
sin. Then He makes them experience the feeling of their corruption: He permits bad thoughts and evil desires of all kinds
to take possession of their minds and their hearts. All their
passions seem to be unchained. The Devil joins his black sug-
gestions to the inclinations of corrupt nature. These souls, in
reality so pure, so full of horror for everything evil, are plunged
into evil and hemmed in by it; they think they have plunged
themselves into it and have surrounded themselves with it,

---

[11] St. Teresa of Avila (1515-1582), Spanish Carmelite nun
and mystic.

through their own fault. They see themselves covered apparently with the most horrible sins; they imagine they have consented to these sins, when in reality they are farther from them than ever. Their director, who knows so well what are their real dispositions, cannot succeed in reassuring them.

God will keep them in this state until they have acquired a humility proportionate to the high degree of sanctity to which He intends to raise them. The lives of many of the greatest saints show us the truth of this, and mystical writers have given rules for the discernment of this state and for the conduct of the favored souls whom God causes to pass through this terrible trial.

St. Paul tells us of himself, that to hinder him from being filled with pride at the greatness of the revelations vouchsafed to him, God gave him a thorn in his flesh, and allowed the angel of Satan to buffet him. And he adds that when he prayed and asked God three times to deliver him from this trial, God answered him, "My grace is sufficient for thee: for my strength is made perfect in weakness";[12] that is to say, that when we feel most deeply our own weakness, it is then that we experience the strength of the divine grace, and it is then that our virtue is really purified.

[12] 2 Cor. 12:7-9.

Chapter Eight

Strive to perfect yourself and to let God perfect you

"From the days of John the Baptist even until now," said our Lord, "the kingdom of Heaven suffereth violence, and the violent take it by force."[13]

In one sense, Jesus Christ has rendered the way to Heaven easier, by the abundant outpouring of His grace and by the spirit of love with which He has replenished His disciples; on the other hand, He has made this way even straiter, because He came to fulfill the law in its perfection, and He requires from His followers more than God required formerly under the law of nature and the law of Moses. Thus, from the moment John the Baptist announced the coming of the Savior, the kingdom of Heaven is to be obtained only through the violence we do to ourselves; we must seize it and carry it, as it were, by assault.

This saying is hard to nature, for it is against nature herself that we must wage war, and this resistance must sometimes be

[13] Matt. 11:12.

"unto blood," without truce or repose. If the service of God consisted only in a certain routine of external devotion, compatible with a life of ease and comfort, with all the allurements of self-love, and with a secret complacency in ourselves and all we do, the number of saints — that is to say, of true Christians, true lovers of the Gospel — would not be so rare, and our condition would be in every respect happier than that of the Jews, to whom God prescribed so many exterior practices from which the law of grace has delivered us.

But for these exterior practices Jesus Christ has substituted interior ones, which are incomparably more difficult and painful. He came not, He said, "to bring peace, but a sword."[14] He puts this sword in the hands of His servants, and He wishes that they should make use of it against themselves, in that circumcision of the heart which mortifies without pity all the inclinations of corrupt nature, even to finally putting it to death and leaving in the heart, thus mortified, no single trace of the old Adam.

Again I say, how hard, how difficult to bear this! So long as it is only a question of saying certain prescribed prayers, of visiting churches, of practicing works of charity, plenty of people can be found to embrace this kind of devotion. A director who requires no more than this is eagerly listened to; he is a man of God; he is a saint. But if he begins to speak of correcting certain defects, of overcoming human respect, of reforming natural character, of keeping a check on natural inclinations and feelings, and of following in everything the leading of grace,

[14] Matt. 10:34.

he is no longer listened to; he exaggerates; he goes further than is necessary.

It is nevertheless certain that the true spirit of Christianity consists in this: that a real Christian should look upon himself as his greatest enemy; that he should wage continual war against himself; that he should spare himself in nothing and count all his progress by the victories he gains over himself.

When a person begins to give himself entirely to God, God treats him at first with great kindness, to win him to Himself. He fills his soul with an ineffable peace and joy. He makes him take delight in solitude, in recollection, and in all his religious duties. He makes the practice of virtue easy to him; nothing is a trouble to him; he thinks he is capable of everything.

∞

God tests everyone who loves Him

But as soon as God is certain of a person's soul, immediately He begins to enlighten him as to his defects; He raises by degrees the veil that concealed them from him, and He inspires him with a firm will to overcome them. From that moment, such a person turns against himself. He undertakes the conquest of self-love; he pursues it relentlessly wherever he perceives it. And when he is thoroughly illuminated by the divine light, where does he not perceive it? He sees in himself nothing but misery, imperfection, sin, self-seeking, and attachment to his own will. His very devotion appears to him full of defects. He once thought he loved God, and now he finds that this love was nothing but another form of self-seeking; that he has appropriated to himself the gifts of God; that he has served

Him only for selfish ends; that he has thought highly of himself and despised others whom he considers not to have received the same graces as himself.

God shows him all this gradually; for if He were to show it to him all at once, he could not bear it and would fall into despair. But the little He does show him is sufficient to convince him that he has not even begun to enter upon the way of perfection and that he has many and many a hard battle to fight before he can arrive at the end of it.

∞

The faithful soul relies completely on God

If the soul is courageous and faithful, what does he do then? He humbles himself, without despairing; he places all his confidence in God; he implores His assistance in the war he is going to undertake. Then he fills his mind and heart with this maxim from the book of the *Imitation of Christ:* "You will make no progress except insofar as you do violence to yourself"[15] — a maxim that contains the purest spirit of the Gospel and that all the saints have followed.

After their example, he also declares war against nature, against his own mind and heart, against his natural character and disposition; and in order that he may not be carried away by imagination or an indiscreet zeal, he begs of God that He will Himself direct him in this war, that He will enlighten him as to the enemies against whom he ought to fight, that He will pass over nothing, but will warn him of all that goes on within

[15] Thomas à Kempis, *Imitation of Christ*, Bk. 3, ch. 39, no. 4.

him, that he may regulate all by the help of His grace. He forms the generous resolution of restraining himself in everything and of allowing nothing in himself that could wound the infinite sanctity of God.

Now he is a true soldier of Jesus Christ; now he is enrolled under His banner. Until now, God has only been preparing and disposing him for this great grace. But from this moment, he is clothed with the armor of faith and enters in good earnest upon the field of battle.

How long shall this conflict last?

It shall last as long as there is one enemy to conquer, as long as nature shall preserve one spark of life, as long as the old Adam is not utterly destroyed.

A good Christian never lays down his arms, and all is not finished for him even when he has fought until his strength is exhausted.

∽

The faithful soul lets God perfect him

What do I mean to express by this? What can remain for him to do when he is worn out by his own victories and when he has carried his violence against himself as far as it can possibly go? There remains nothing for him to *do*, but there remains for him to *suffer* the action of God, who henceforth will do alone what is beyond the strength of man.

Sanctity is begun by our own efforts and sustained and assisted by divine grace: it is finished and perfected solely by the divine operation. Man raises the edifice as high as he can, but because there is a great deal that is human in this edifice, God destroys all the work of man and substitutes for it His own work, and the creature has nothing else to do but to allow the Creator to act as He pleases. The creature acts no more, but he suffers, because God is acting upon him; he no longer uses violence toward himself, but he suffers it; and this purely passive state is immeasurably more painful. As long as the soul is acting, there is always the consciousness of strength, and that consciousness is sustaining. Also, in the consciousness of strength there is always a little self-love, and the person can scarcely help attributing to himself some share in the victory, since he has indeed contributed to it.

But when God acts alone, every faculty of action is taken from the soul. The person sees perfectly what God is doing in him, but he cannot second Him; and it is no trouble to him now to attribute nothing to himself, because he sees plainly that he has no part in it. Besides, all the work of God then consists in destroying, in overturning, in despoiling the soul and reducing it to a perfect emptiness and nakedness. And He demands of the person no other correspondence than that he should patiently allow himself to be despoiled of all the gifts, all the graces, and all the virtues with which God had adorned him and which he had appropriated to himself.

Oh, what a great and difficult work is this total destruction, this annihilation, of the creature! What a warfare to sustain for so many long years! And then, when we think all is finished, to have to bear new and far more terrible blows from the hand of God Himself, who acts upon His creature as the sovereign Master and exercises upon him all the authority he freely gave Him by renouncing his liberty to Him! What courage is necessary to undertake and bring to a final conclusion the war against ourselves! But what a far greater courage is necessary to bear the war that God Himself wages against us and to allow ourselves to be crushed under the blows of His all-powerful hand!

> *O my God, now I begin to understand*
> *what that violence is that he whom Thou*
> *dost call to the perfection of Thy holy gospel*
> *must do to himself and must experience.*
> *But thanks be to Thine infinite mercy,*
> *this sight does not frighten me.*
> *If I relied on myself, I would give up all,*
> *because I feel that I am capable of nothing!*
> *But I rely on Thee alone, and "I can do*
> *all things in Him who strengtheneth me."*[16]
> *Thou hast begun the work, and my ardent hope*
> *is that Thou wilt continue it and finish it.*
> *I wish to have no other part in it*
> *than to cooperate with Thee as much as I am able*
> *and then to leave Thee to do with me as Thou wilt.*

[16] Phil. 4:13.

Chapter Nine

∞

Know what God asks of you and what you should ask of God

It is very important — it is absolutely necessary — in our spiritual life that we should be able to distinguish clearly, with regard to our interior dispositions, between what God actually asks of us and what we ought to ask of God — or, rather, between what He has a right to expect from us and what He wishes us to expect from Him. For the want of clear discernment in these two things, we often fall into trying doubts and perplexities about our state. We are discontented with ourselves when there is no occasion to be so, or we are delighted with ourselves, and think God is delighted with us, when He is not. We complain of the designs of Providence and murmur against them unjustly. In the end, we commit many faults and expose ourselves to the danger of giving up everything.

Let us try, then, by the light of truth, to distinguish between these two things and to fix each one clearly in our minds, so that we may be able to make of them afterward the rule of our judgments and the guide of our conduct.

The Spiritual Life

∞
God asks us to be
ever attentive to His grace

God asks from us only what it depends on ourselves to give. This principle is self-evident. Now, only one single thing depends on us, and that is the good use of our liberty, according to the actual measure of grace that is enlightening our mind and exciting our will.

God, then, asks of us, in the first place, a constant attention to what is passing in our own hearts and to His voice, which speaks to us there. This constant attention is not so difficult as we might think, if we love God sincerely and are determined to please Him in all things.

He asks of us that we shall never give ourselves up to anything that can distract us from this attention, whether it be exterior amusement, or curiosity, or undue attachment to any object, or useless thoughts, or voluntary trouble and agitation of mind, from any cause whatever. He also asks that when we notice that anything in particular has the power to distract us from this attention to the voice of grace, we shall at once give up that thing and put it away from us.

But we must not imagine that either the duties of our state of life, or domestic troubles, or the ordinary events of every day, or the courtesy we owe to society can of themselves injure this interior recollection; we can preserve it in the midst of all these things.

And, besides, after we have used a little violence toward ourselves for a time, this recollection becomes so natural that we scarcely perceive it, and seldom or ever lose it.

∾

God asks us to cooperate with His grace

God asks of us a full, perfect, and faithful correspondence
to grace, in all circumstances in which we may find ourselves.
The grace of beginners is not the same as that of those who are
more advanced, and the grace of those who are advanced is
not the same as that of those who are consummated in the way
of perfection. A disposition that is good in a beginner is not
so in one who is more advanced; such and such a practice is
proper for one state and would not be so for another. We must,
then, understand how to take them up and leave them, following the instinct of grace, and not to attach ourselves to any
one of them with any kind of obstinacy. Still less must we desire to raise ourselves above our present state, until God Himself raises us; nor must we undertake or wish for what is beyond
our strength or imagine we can do what we admire in the
saints, or think we may allow ourselves certain liberties that
God grants only to those souls who have passed through every
sort of trial.

∾

God asks us to be faithful to Him

God asks of us that when we have given ourselves to Him,
we shall never take ourselves away from Him in anything; that
we shall never act on our own responsibility, but always consult Him in everything, and also those guides whom He has
given us to direct us, especially when we wish to do anything
extraordinary. He asks that we shall remain passive and submissive to His will in any state in which it pleases Him to place

us; that we shall never do anything of ourselves to go out of this state, on the pretext that it is too painful for human nature and that we cannot bear it any longer. We must not ask Him to deliver us from a temptation, or a humiliation, or an interior trial, if He wills that we should be tempted, or humiliated, or tried for our greater purification; but we must ask of Him the courage and strength to bear it to the end.

∞

God asks us to abandon ourselves to Him

What God asks of us, above all things, is the entire resignation and abandonment of ourselves to Him — a resignation of all without exception and forever. But as this abandonment has its degrees, and goes on increasing, until in the end we lose ourselves utterly in Him, we have simply to keep ourselves in a general disposition to sacrifice to Him each thing as He asks it of us and, when the occasion presents itself, to make the actual sacrifice.

There is, then, no necessity to anticipate anything or to imagine ourselves in circumstances where, perhaps, we shall never be or to exhaust our strength beforehand by wondering if we could bear such and such a trial. All this is useless and even dangerous — useless, because we never can foresee the future or form a just idea of any situation, whether interior or exterior, in which we may be placed; and dangerous, because by such thoughts we expose ourselves to presumption or to discouragement. Entire resignation of self leaves to God the care of the future, and occupies itself only with the present moment.

God does not ask of us either sensible devotion or those great lights and fine sentiments on which self-love feeds too much. These graces depend on Him alone; He gives them and takes them away when He pleases. There is, then, no necessity for being desolate and miserable if we have no sensible devotion at prayer or Holy Communion — if we are dry, stupid, heavy, or incapable of any pious feeling. Still less must we think that prayer and Communion made like this is worth nothing. Self-love might so judge, but God judges differently.

God does not ask that we keep our imagination captive in such a manner that we are absolutely masters of our thoughts. This does not depend on us; but it does depend on us never willfully to dwell on thoughts that disturb our peace, to despise them, not to allow them to trouble and torment us, and in this, as in all else, to be guided by the decisions of our spiritual director.

It does not depend on us, either, to be free from temptations against purity, against faith or hope. These are temptations that God may permit for our greater advancement. We may ask submissively, as St. Paul did, to be delivered from them; but if God answers us, as He answered St. Paul, "My grace is sufficient for thee,"[17] we must bear these temptations with humility and fight against them as well as we can, using the means prescribed by obedience.

In those events that depend on Providence or the will of others, God asks of us entire submission and that we should try to draw from them as much profit as possible, for His glory and

[17] 2 Cor. 12:9.

our own sanctification, being persuaded, as St. Paul says, that "all things work together for good to them that love God."[18]

❧

God asks us to be diligent in all we do

With regard to all our undertakings, even the most holy, in which we are engaged by the will of God, He asks of us only our faithful labor, our careful application, and the employment of the means in our power. But He does not ask of us success; that depends on Him alone. And sometimes He permits, for our greater good, that the success should not be according to our hopes and intentions.

❧

Ask God for what will lead to your salvation

This is in some slight degree, and briefly, what God asks of us and what depends on the good use of our free will. As to what we must ask of God, it is quite certain that we are not fit judges as to what is best for us or what would harm us, and we cannot do better than to leave it entirely to God. Our best plan is, then, to keep in general to what the law teaches that we must necessarily ask for and to observe a holy indifference with regard to all those things which are not absolutely necessary to our perfection.

• *Self-knowledge*. One thing we must ask is that we may know God and know ourselves; what He is and what we

---

[18] Rom. 8:28.

are; what He has done for us and what we have done against Him; what He deserves and what He has a right to require of us; the value of His grace and the importance of making good use of it.

• *Trust.* We must ask for a perfect and entire trust in Him, a trust that will reach so far as to make us say with holy Job, "Though He slay me, yet will I trust in Him."[19]

• *Devotion.* We must ask that we may love and serve God, at the expense of any sacrifice of ourselves, without the slightest regard for our own interest, solely for His glory and the accomplishment of His good pleasure.

• *Faith.* We must ask for the spirit of faith, which will raise us above all testimony, above all assurance, above all reason; that is to say, our faith will rest, not on human testimony, not on any mere feeling of assurance, not on mere reason, but simply and solely on the will of God, as revealed to His Church. And this bare and simple faith will sustain us in the most obscure darkness, in the deprivation of all sensible support, and will keep us in profound peace, although we may feel as if suspended between Heaven and Hell.

• *Obedience.* We must ask for a spirit of blind obedience, which will make us die to our own judgment and our own will, which will make us act against what appears to be reason and our own natural aversions, which will

[19] Job 13:15.

allow us neither to reflect nor to reason, because it is certain that the ways of God are above all our thoughts and contrary to all our natural inclinations and that we shall never advance in the way of perfection until we cast ourselves blindly and without reserve into what may appear to us at first as an abyss, unfathomable and without resource.

Chapter Ten

∞

Rely completely on God

St. Paul said, "When I am weak, then I am strong."[20] That is to say, when I have a clear conviction of my weakness; when I know it thoroughly by my own experience; when, seeing that of myself I can do nothing, I humble myself and put all my trust in God, it is then that I am strong with the strength of God, who delights in making His power shine forth through the weakness of His creature; it is then that I can do all things through Him who strengthens me.[21]

No less true is it that when we are strong with our own strength, we are really weak. That is to say, when we think ourselves strong, when we take to ourselves the credit of this strength, when we presume upon it, when we are proud of it and think ourselves capable of doing everything and suffering everything, it is then that we are really weak, because God takes away His strength from His presumptuous creature and abandons him to himself.

[20] 2 Cor. 12:10.
[21] Cf. Phil. 4:13.

The Spiritual Life

∞

God teaches us to rely solely on Him

Strength in ourselves is, then, a real weakness, and even an extreme weakness; it is an inevitable cause of falls, and almost always of the most humiliating falls. On the contrary, weakness in ourselves, if it is accompanied by humility and trust in God, is a real strength, an all-powerful strength, even the strength of God Himself.

But why does God wish us to be penetrated by this conviction of our own weakness? It is so that He may make His strength shine forth in us. It is because He wishes that all the good in us should be attributed to Him alone; it is because He wishes to be recognized as the sole Author and the sole Finisher of all human sanctity; it is because He cannot endure in the order of grace above all things that the creature should think he can of himself do the least thing, or that he should depend on himself, on his own resolutions, his own courage, or his own dispositions.

The great secret of the conduct of God toward a soul He wishes to sanctify is, then, to take from that soul every kind of confidence in itself. And to do this, He begins by delivering the person up, as it were, to all his misery. He allows every arrangement he makes by his own judgment to deceive all his hopes. He allows all his ideas and projects to fail. He allows his understanding to lead him astray and his judgment to deceive him. He allows his foresight to be in vain and his will to be feeble. He allows him to fall at every step. He wishes to teach him never to rely on himself in anything, but to rely only on Him.

Rely completely on God

When we begin to serve God, when we experience the sensible effects of grace, when our mind is illuminated by a great light and our will is transported by holy emotions, it is quite natural that we should think we are capable of doing everything and suffering everything for God; we cannot imagine that we could ever refuse Him anything, or even that we could hesitate ever so little in the most difficult things. Sometimes, even, we go so far as to ask for great crosses or great humiliations, persuaded that we are quite strong enough to bear them.

If our soul is upright and simple, this kind of presumption, born of the intense realization we have of the strength of grace, comes only from want of experience and does not displease God, provided it is not accompanied by a great opinion of ourselves and a vain feeling of complacency in ourselves.

But God is not slow in curing the soul of this good opinion of itself. He has only to withdraw His sensible grace, to leave the soul to itself, to expose it to a very light temptation. At once the person feels disgust and repugnance. He sees everywhere obstacles and difficulties. He succumbs to the smallest temptations; a look, a gesture, a word throws him off his guard — he who thought himself superior to the greatest dangers.

Now he passes to the opposite extreme: he fears everything; he despairs of everything; he thinks he can never overcome himself in anything; he is tempted to abandon everything. In fact, he would give up all, if God did not quickly come to his assistance. God continues this method with regard to the soul until, by reiterated experiences, He has well convinced the person of his own nothingness, of his utter incapacity of all good, and of the absolute necessity of leaning on Him alone.

To this end, He allows temptations to come upon him, so that a hundred times he sees himself ready to yield, if God does not come to his assistance, when there is no other resource. He allows the revolt of passions that the person thought were forever extinguished and that suddenly rise up with an extreme violence, obscuring the reason and bringing the soul to the very brink of ruin. He expressly allows him to fall into every kind of human weakness, in order to humble him. He allows strange repugnances and difficulties in the practice of virtue, a strong aversion for prayer and the other exercises of piety. In a word, He gives that person's soul a clear vision of his own natural malignity and aversion for good. God employs all these means to annihilate the soul in its own eyes, to inspire it with hatred and horror for itself, to convince the person that there is no crime too horrible for him to be guilty of, and not the least good action, not the least effort, not the faintest good desire, nor the smallest good thought that he is capable of producing by himself.

∞

Sorrows and faults help you to rely on God
When, at last, after many blows, many falls, many miseries, the soul is finally reduced to such a state that it relies no longer on itself in the smallest thing, then God clothes it by degrees with His own strength, always making it feel that this strength is not in itself, but comes simply from above. And when the soul has this real strength, the person can undertake all; he can bear all: sufferings, humiliations of every kind, labors and troubles for the glory of God and the good of others. He

succeeds in everything; no difficulty stops him, no obstacle resists him, no danger frightens him, because it is no longer himself — it is God who is acting and suffering in him. Not only does he give God all the glory, but he recognizes and knows by experience that God alone does all, and can do all, and that he is nothing but a feeble instrument in His hands, to be moved by His will, or rather, that he is an abyss of nothingness that He deigns to employ for the execution of His designs.

It is thus that St. Paul, after having related all the great things he had done and suffered for the gospel, adds with the most intense conviction, "Nevertheless, I am nothing; it was not I, but the grace of God, which is in me."[22]

Such a person renders to God all the glory He expects from him and reserves absolutely nothing for himself, because he looks on himself as he really is, and that is nothingness. Thus, he glorifies God in two ways: by all he does and suffers for Him, and by this interior disposition of annihilation.

Oh, how dead we must be to ourselves, through how many trials must we have passed, to attain this! But, then, when we have attained it, our life is one long canticle of praise. God Himself is praised and glorified in such a soul; all is there for Him; there is no self left.

∞

Learn to be strong with the strength of God
But what must we do to succeed in being thus strong with the strength of God? Of course, the determination must be

---

[22] Cf. 1 Cor. 15:10.

firm and unshaken to refuse nothing to God and to do nothing deliberate that may displease Him. When this foundation is well laid, I say that we must humble ourselves for our faults, but never allow them to trouble us, looking on them as a proof of our own weakness and drawing from them the fruit God wishes us to draw from them, which is never to trust in ourselves, but always and only in Him.

Then we must not think too much of the good sentiments that come to us in certain times of fervor, nor must we think ourselves better and stronger than we really are because of these passing emotions. The only time to judge ourselves rightly is when sensible grace is withdrawn from us.

Also, we must never be discouraged by the sight of our own misery, nor must we say, "No, I can never do or suffer such and such a thing." But while we confess that we are of ourselves incapable of the least effort of virtue, let us always say, "God is all powerful. As long as I lean only on Him, He will make easy and possible for me those things which seem beyond my strength." We must say to God, like St. Augustine, "Give what Thou commandest, and command what Thou pleasest."

We must not be astonished at any disinclination we feel in ourselves, but we must incessantly ask of God the grace to raise us above it. And when we have overcome ourselves in anything, we must not take the credit of the victory to ourselves, but thank God for it.

Finally, we must be neither presumptuous nor cowardly — two faults that arise, one from trusting too much in ourselves, and the other from not trusting enough in God. Cowardice comes from a want of faith; presumption from an insufficient knowledge of ourselves. How can we be presumptuous if we are convinced that our strength comes from elsewhere? How can we be cowardly if we believe, as we ought to believe, that our strength is the very strength of the Almighty?

∞

Chapter Eleven

Use your time wisely

The greater number of mankind employ their time badly; many others are perfectly embarrassed by their time and do not know how to employ it; their sole object is to fritter it away, to pass it agreeably to themselves, or at least without feeling themselves wearied and bored.

Do they ever succeed in this? No. Experience teaches us that those people who are most greedy for pleasure are soon satiated with it, and that disgust, weariness, and idleness soon render them unbearable, even to themselves. But unfortunately, when they have acquired this experience, it is very rarely that they profit by it: the bad habits are formed; it would cost too much to adopt good ones. They continue to live as they have lived, although they no longer flatter themselves with the hope of the happiness they once confidently expected. Woe to those who abuse and misuse their time! One day they will regret having acted so, but then their regrets will be in vain.

Let us now propose for Christians and interior souls some salutary and useful reflections.

The Spiritual Life

∽

Our use of time will determine our eternity

What is time, with regard to myself? It is my present and actual existence. Past time, or my past existence, is no longer anything, as far as I am concerned; I can neither recall it, nor change anything in it. The time to come, or my future existence, has not yet arrived, and perhaps never will arrive. It does not depend on me; I cannot count on it; and the most powerful monarch in the world cannot make sure of one single instant of life.

No one is ignorant of these two simple truths, but very few draw from them the conclusions they ought to draw.

It is true and certain that I have only the present moment, which cannot be divided, which nothing can fix, not even thought, and which is passing away with a rapidity that nothing can equal.

This present moment, or this actual existence — from whom do I hold it? From God. It is He who called me from nothing into being. It is He who has preserved my existence from one instant to another, and who is preserving it at this present moment. Will He preserve it for me in the moment that shall immediately follow this one? I do not know; and nothing in the world can give me the assurance of it.

Why has time been given to me? So that by it I may merit a happy eternity. I shall live forever: faith teaches me this; my reason even assures me of another life. The desire of immortality is implanted in the depths of my heart, and this desire, which God Himself has planted there, can never be frustrated of its object.

I am, then, born for eternity, but this eternity will be happy or wretched, according to the use I make of time. If I sincerely repent of the bad use of time I have made in the past, if I am beginning to make a good use of it, if I persevere in this good use until the moment comes when time shall cease for me, I shall be eternally happy. If I have made a bad use of time in the past, if I am still doing so, if I continue to do so, and death surprises me in this state, I shall be eternally miserable.

My fate for all eternity depends, then, on the use I make of time, and since neither the past nor the future is in my own power, it is quite true to say that my eternity depends always on the present moment.

Now, at this present moment, what is my state? Would I like to die just as I am now? Would I dare to run the risk of my eternity just as I am now? If I would not, am I not a fool to remain in the state I am in, to count on the future, when I am not sure of the moment that shall follow this one, when perhaps between me and eternity there is only an instant of time?

All the events of life, except sin, can contribute to my happy eternity. It is sin alone that can make me lose it. And what is sin? It is the result of a moment's determination. As soon as the deliberate intention of mortal sin is formed by my will, whether the exterior act follows or not, if I die in that state, I am lost forever, and without resource; and I have no assurance that I shall not die as soon as this deliberate intention to sin is formed in my heart. What folly, then, to consent to that which can ruin me forever, at the very moment I give the consent of my will, even before I have passed to the exterior act of sin!

The Spiritual Life

All the other evils that may happen to us in time are only evils belonging to time itself, and they are evils that may be converted into blessings for all eternity, if we will accept them all as a Christian should and make a holy use of them. We need not fear them so much, and we need not torment ourselves so much to avoid them or to remedy them. Sin alone is the evil that lasts for all eternity; it is an evil that we can never be sure of remedying once we have committed it; it is an evil that can be cured only by repentance, but by a repentance that perhaps may never be in our power and certainly will not be unless God Himself, by granting us more time, gives us, through His infinite goodness alone, the grace of conversion.

∞

Learn to make good use of time
From these deep and serious reflections, it is easy for me to conclude what sort of employment I ought to make of time:

  • Never to do anything that may expose me to the danger of forfeiting my happy eternity;

  • To make of each moment the use that God wishes me to make of it, so that by it I may merit that happy eternity;

  • Never to put off to a moment that perhaps may never come to me what I can and ought to do at the present moment;

  • Never to give to any frivolous amusement, still less to any dangerous amusement, to any useless occupation, or to simple idleness, the time whose moments are so precious;

• To be convinced that a life that may finish at any moment, which has been given to me only so that by it I may merit eternal happiness, ought to be a very serious life, a life divided between the duties I owe to God, to my state, and to society; a life in which I do not seek for any other rest and recreation than what God Himself allows and authorizes, so that this very rest and innocent enjoyment may be another means toward gaining that blessed eternity.

What a reform there would be in the world, and what a difference, if everyone would be guided by these solid truths, on which depend our greatest and only real interest! These rules are for the generality of Christians.

∞

Let God direct your use of time

But with regard to interior souls, there is more than this. They must never look on time as a thing they may dispose of as they will; they must never think they are masters of one single instant. Since they have given themselves entirely to God, their liberty and the use they ought to make of it belong solely to Him, at every instant of their lives. It is for Him to inspire them from one moment to another as to what they have to do, for Him to regulate all their interior dispositions, their exterior acts, and even their innocent amusements. He has become the Master of all that, by the gift they have made Him of themselves. They would take back that gift if they were to make one step, if they were to speak one word, of themselves, without consulting Him.

There is no longer any constraint for them in this; on the contrary, God treats them as His own children; and as long as He knows that their hearts are His alone, He allows them to enjoy a sweet liberty that mere servants know not of.

The only use these souls should make of time is to be attentive each moment to what God asks of them and to be faithful to accomplish it. With the exception of this attention and this fidelity, which soon become a habit with them, they are free from all other care whatsoever. And God, who is the sole Master of their time, disposes of it Himself just as He pleases. There is no longer any necessity for them to trouble themselves about what employment God wishes them to undertake. There is no need for them to form plans for the future; God will provide for that. He will not suffer them to be idle for a moment; He will arrange everything; He will direct everything. And even if He gives them no exterior occupation, He will keep them interiorly occupied with Himself.

Even if a spiritual life had no other advantage than this, that it keeps us in perfect repose as to the employment of our time and gives us a calm assurance that all our moments are employed according to the will of God, that alone is an inestimable advantage, which we can never buy too dearly.

The sole object of the interior soul is to glorify God, to love God; to glorify Him by all his actions and by all his sufferings, which come to him through His choice and in which he has nothing to do but patiently to submit; to love Him, not by formal acts or by effusions of sensible devotion, but by being effectually and continually devoted to Him, and by an entire resignation of his own will to His.

This, from one moment to another, and without any interruption, is the constant occupation of that favored soul. The person's exterior situation may change; he may pass from repose to action, from health to sickness; he may experience every sort of vicissitude from within and without. In this, as all others are, he is subject to the changes of time. But the depths of his heart are changeless as God Himself, and fixed in a constant peace, except that his union with God goes on increasing, and becomes closer and closer, as time goes on.

In this respect, time has almost ceased to exist for him; he is almost transported to eternity. Yes, from the moment that he gave himself entirely to God, so long as he does not take back that gift, so long as he remains in that state of simple dependence on God's will and never swerves from that dependence by any deliberate act, he participates, in the depths of his being, in the very being of God, because he is every moment just what God wishes him to be. He works and acts as a creature, but God works and acts with him as a Creator. And as this divine action is continual, and as he is always submissive to it, he is, notwithstanding occasional miseries and weaknesses, already on this earth in a peace that is almost like that of the blessed in Heaven; and the changes of time no longer affect him, any more than they affect God, because they are incapable of altering the fixed disposition of his heart.

Happy are those who understand this; happier still are those who faithfully practice it!

Chapter Twelve

∽

Learn to profit from your faults

Deriving profit from our faults is one of the most important topics in the spiritual life. It is quite certain that, in the designs of God, the faults into which He permits us to fall ought to serve for our sanctification, and that it depends on us to draw this advantage from them.

Nevertheless, it happens, on the contrary, that our faults themselves do us less harm than does the bad use we make of them.

What I have to say on this subject has nothing to do with those cowardly souls who use reserve with God and who wish to belong to Him only up to a certain point. They commit deliberately and knowingly a thousand faults, from which it is impossible to draw any profit, on account of the bad dispositions in which they are. The persons for whom I write are those who have made up their minds never deliberately and with intention to commit a single fault, and who nevertheless do fall into many faults, in spite of their good resolutions, through inadvertence, or on the impulse of the moment, or through weakness.

The Spiritual Life

∽

Do not be surprised or discouraged by your falls

To these persons it generally happens that they are astonished at their faults, that they are troubled by them, that they are ashamed of them, and so are angry with themselves and fall into discouragement. These are just so many effects of self-love, effects far more pernicious than the faults themselves. We are astonished that we should have fallen; but we are quite wrong, and it is a sign that we know nothing whatever about ourselves. We ought, on the contrary, to be surprised that we do not fall much more often and into much more grievous faults, and we ought to give thanks to God for all the falls from which He preserves us. We are troubled every time we discover some fault in ourselves. We lose our interior peace; we are quite agitated, and we occupy ourselves about this fault for hours, or even for whole days.

Now, we ought never to be troubled; but when we see ourselves on the ground, we must raise ourselves up again quietly. At once we must turn to God with love and humility and ask His pardon; and then we must never think about the fault again, until the time comes to accuse ourselves of it in Confession. And even if in Confession we forget it, there is no occasion to be uneasy on that account.

Or again, we are so ashamed of our faults that we hardly dare to tell them to our confessor. "What will he think of me, after so many promises, after so many good resolutions I have made in his presence?" If you declare your faults to him simply and humbly, he will only think the better of you; if you tell them to him with difficulty and reserve, he cannot help taxing you with pride in his own mind. His confidence in you will diminish as he sees that you are not sufficiently open with him.

But the worst of all is this: we are vexed with ourselves; we are angry, as St. Francis de Sales[23] says, at having been angry; we are impatient at having been impatient. What misery! Ought we not to see that this is pride pure and simple; that we are humiliated at finding ourselves, when put to the proof, less strong and less holy than we thought we were; and that we aspire to be exempt from faults and imperfections only so that we may take credit for it and so that we may be able to congratulate ourselves on having passed a day or a week without having anything to reproach ourselves with?

Finally, we grow discouraged. We give up all our practices of piety, one after the other. We give up prayer; we regard perfection as impossible, and we despair of ever attaining it. What is the use, we ask, of restraining ourselves, of watching continually over ourselves, of giving ourselves up to recollection and mortification, when we grow no better, when we correct nothing and are always falling afresh?

Now, this is one of the most subtle snares of the Devil. And do you wish to be preserved from it? Then you must never be discouraged, no matter into how many faults you fall; but you must say to yourself, "If I should fall twenty times, a hundred times, a day, I will get up again every time, and I will go on my way." What will it matter, after all, how many times you have fallen on the way if you reach your journey's end safely at last? God will not reproach you.

[23] St. Francis de Sales (1567-1622), Bishop of Geneva.

The Spiritual Life

Often our very falls come from the rapidity of our course and because the ardor that impels us scarcely gives us time to take certain precautions.

Those timid and overly cautious souls who always wish to see where they are putting their feet, who are always turning out of the way to avoid making a false step, and who are dreadfully afraid of contracting the least stain will not advance half so fast as the other, more generous souls, and death often overtakes them before their course is run. It is not those who commit the fewest faults who are the holiest, but those who have the most courage, the most generosity, and the most love, who make the greatest efforts, and who are not afraid of stumbling a little, or even of falling and staining themselves a little, provided they can always advance.

∞

Our faults can lead us closer to God

St. Paul says that "all things work together for good to them that love God."[24] Yes, everything is for their good, even their faults, and sometimes even their grave faults. God permits those very faults to cure us of vain presumption, to teach us what we really are and of what we are really capable. David confessed that the adultery and murder of which he was guilty had served to keep him in a continual distrust of himself. "It is good for me," he said to God, "that Thou hast humbled me; I have been more faithful in keeping Thy commandments."[25]

[24] Rom. 8:28.
[25] Cf. Ps. 118:71 (RSV = Ps. 119:71).

Learn to profit from your faults

The fall of St. Peter was for him the most useful of lessons, and the humility with which it inspired him disposed him to receive the gifts of the Holy Spirit, to become the Head of the Church, and they preserved him from the dangers of so eminent a position. St. Paul, in the great success of his apostolate, preserved himself from pride and vainglory by remembering how he had once been a blasphemer and a persecutor of the Church of God. And more than this, a humiliating temptation, from which God would not deliver him, served as a balance to the sublimity of the revelations granted to him.[26]

If God was able to draw such an advantage from even the greatest sins, who can doubt that He will make our daily faults serve for our sanctification? Many masters of the spiritual life have remarked that God often leaves in the most holy souls certain defects, from which, notwithstanding all their efforts, they cannot free themselves entirely, to make them feel their own weakness and what they would be without His grace, to hinder them from being proud of the favors He grants them, and to dispose them to receive these favors with more humility — in short, to nourish in them a certain disgust with themselves, and so to protect them against all the snares of self-love; to animate their fervor and keep them in a constant state of watchfulness, of trust in God and perseverance in prayer. The child who falls when he has gone a little way from his mother and wishes to walk alone, returns to her with more affection, to be cured of the hurt he has given himself, and he learns by that fall to leave her no more. The experience of his own

[26] 2 Cor. 12:7-9.

weakness, and of the tenderness with which his mother received him, makes him love her more than ever.

∽

Faults can be occasions for practicing virtue

The faults that happen to us often give us occasion for great acts of virtue, which we certainly would not have had the opportunity of practicing without them; and God allows these faults with that intention. For instance, He permits a flash of ill-natured sarcasm, an act of rudeness, or a lively impatience so that we may at once make an act of humility that abundantly satisfies for our fault and the scandal it may have given.

The fault was committed on the impulse of the moment, but the act of reparation is made with reflection, with an effort over ourselves, with a full and deliberate will. This is an act that pleases God much more than the fault displeased Him.

God also makes use of our faults and apparent imperfections to conceal our sanctity from the eyes of others and to procure for us humiliations from them.

God is a great and wise Master. Let Him do as He likes; He will not fail in His work. Let us make up our minds carefully to avoid everything that can displease Him the least in the world. But if we should fall into any fault, let us be sorry on His account and not on our own. Let us love the humiliation into which this fault throws us; let us beg of God to draw from our humiliation His glory. He will do this and, by this means, will advance us far more than by a life apparently more regular and holy, but which would destroy our self-love less efficaciously.

Learn to profit from your faults

When God asks of us to do certain things, let us never draw back on the pretense of fearing the faults we may commit in executing His wishes. It is better to do good, even with imperfection, than to omit it. Sometimes we do not administer a necessary correction because we are afraid of doing it with too much severity, or we avoid associating with certain persons because their faults try us so much and make us feel so impatient and irritable. But how shall we acquire virtue if we fly from the occasions of practicing it? Is not such a flight a greater fault than the faults we fear to fall into?

Let us take care only to have a good intention; then let us go wherever duty calls us, and let us be sure that God is kind enough and indulgent enough to pardon us all the faults to which His faithful service and the desire of pleasing Him may expose us.

Chapter Thirteen

∞

Do not be discouraged by temptations

"Because you were pleasing to God," said the angel Raphael to Tobias, "it was needful that you should be tried by temptation."[27] Those who have given themselves up to the spiritual life have no difficulty in persuading themselves that they are pleasing to God, when He makes them feel the sweetness of His presence, when He overwhelms them with His caresses, when they enjoy a peace that nothing seems to trouble, and when they experience nothing painful either from the attacks of the Devil or from the malice of man.

But when God withdraws His consolations, when He allows the Devil to tempt them and men to put their virtue to the proof, then, if they are told that all this is a certain sign that they are pleasing to God, it would not be so easy to persuade them of it. On the contrary, they think that God has forsaken them, that they please Him no longer as they once did, and they seek uneasily to discover what there can have been in their conduct to induce God to treat them with so much severity.

[27] Tob. 12:13.

The Spiritual Life

Nevertheless, here is an angel revealing to Tobias that it was just because he was pleasing to God that it was necessary for him to be tried by temptation. Mark the connection: God, the Devil, and men all try you. What is the necessary cause of this treatment? It is because you are pleasing to God. Temptations are therefore the reward of your previous fidelity; and God allows them on purpose to make you still more agreeable in His eyes, and consequently more holy and perfect. Every page of the Old and the New Testament contains proofs and examples of this truth. It is undoubtedly the most powerful motive for consolation that the servants of God can have in all their trials.

Thus, when they begin to give themselves to God, the first thing they must most certainly expect is this: if they serve Him with their whole heart, if they are faithful to His graces, if they neglect nothing to make themselves pleasing in His sight, He will try them with every sort of affliction. He will allow the Devil to tempt them; He will send them humiliations and persecutions; and they must prepare themselves for all this by an entire resignation to the will of God.

But if, after several years have passed in the service of God, their interior peace is uncrossed by any kind of trouble, if the Devil and men leave them in tranquility, then it is that they ought to mistrust their virtue and believe that they are not really as pleasing to God as they thought they were.

&

Temptation proves the genuineness of virtue
It is, therefore, very necessary that temptation should try the true servants of God. What do we mean by the word *try?*

Do not be discouraged by temptations

We mean, first, that temptation makes clear and obvious the truth and genuineness of their virtue. For what is a virtue worth that has never been exercised? It is a feeble virtue, a doubtful virtue of which we can make no account and which we cannot rely on. Is it at all difficult to walk when God is helping us on? Or to pray when we are inundated with spiritual consolations? Or to overcome ourselves when the attractions of grace are so triumphant that they leave scarcely any room for the smallest resistance on the part of nature? Is it a painful thing to rest peacefully in the bosom of God, sheltered from all winds and tempests; to be feared by the Devil, who keeps himself at a distance, and respected by men who pay homage to piety in our person?

Certainly holiness would be neither difficult, nor rare, nor terrible to corrupt nature, if it could be acquired without any effort, without any combats, without any contradictions. And it would have been most unreasonable of St. Paul to compare Christians to the athletes who, after long and painful training, came to struggle in the arena and gained the victory at the cost of so much sweat and often of so much blood. A virtue that has never been tried does not deserve the name of virtue.

∞

Temptation purifies virtue

Next, what does *try* mean? It means to purify. Just as metals are tried and purified from all alloy when they are placed in a crucible, so is virtue purified in the crucible of temptation. And from what is it purified? From the alloy of that spirit of self-interest that debases it, from the self-love that corrupts it, and from the pride that poisons it. It is impossible for virtue to be what it should be — that is to say, disinterested, unappropriating, expecting no reward, free from all vain complacency — unless it has passed through the crucible of many temptations. The effect of every temptation against purity, for example, or against faith, or against hope is to strengthen these virtues in our soul and carry them to the highest degree. The effect of anxieties, of weariness, of doing good, of disgust at everything, of evident repugnance to duty, of extreme desolation, so that all sensible grace is withdrawn from us, and God seems to have forsaken us — the effect of all this is to purify our love, to increase our courage, our fidelity, and our perseverance. The effect of calumnies, vexations, and persecutions is to raise us above all human respect, and at the same time to take away from us a certain good opinion of ourselves that the praise of men nourishes in us without our perceiving it. Finally, the general effect of all temptations is to detach us from the things of this world, to humble us in our own eyes, to inspire us with more trust in God, and to draw us into closer union with Him.

Temptations are entirely, therefore, in the designs of God — the recompense, the proof, and the consummation of virtue. How, after that, can we fear them? If humility does not allow us to desire them, because that would be to presume on our own strength, the zeal for our perfection also does not allow to dread them, still less to be unhappy when they do come and to think that all is lost.

But you may say, "I am so afraid of sinning, I am so afraid of forfeiting grace, I am so afraid of being lost, and I see myself exposed by temptation to the danger of all this." You may as well say that you are afraid of fighting, of gaining the victory, and of being crowned; for the apostle says that the crown of glory is destined only for those who have fought according to the rules.[28]

❦

Trust in God's strength

Do you not see that this very fear of sinning, which makes you so weak and cowardly, comes from your only considering your own strength, and not thinking enough of the help of God, which can render you invincible? I grant you that if you look only at your own weakness, the least temptation may be strong enough to overcome you.

Therefore, you ought never to look at yourself, except to acknowledge and distrust your own weakness; you ought to throw yourself into the arms of God, so that He may be your support and your protection. Can you be afraid of sinning when the arm of the All-Powerful sustains you? What can the strength of all men and all devils do against Him? Can they tear you from His arms without your consent? Is not His help assured to you in all those temptations that He permits, which you have not sought of yourself, in which you mistrust your own strength, and to which you have exposed yourself only at His command?

Listen to the words of St. Paul; it is to you that he speaks: "God is faithful," he says. "He will not suffer you to be tempted

---

[28] Cf. 2 Tim. 4:8.

above what you are able to bear; but will, with the temptation, also make a way to escape, that you may be able to bear it."[29] Weigh well these words, for they will fill you with consolation and confidence in the midst of the hardest trial. "God is faithful": He owes it to Himself, He owes it to His own promises, He owes it to His love for you, to succor you in any danger that threatens your soul. His glory is interested in helping you, because sin is an offense against Him. He knows that you can do nothing without Him and that you will most certainly fall if He abandons you. If He failed you in these critical moments, He would not be Himself.

"He will not suffer you to be tempted above what you are able to bear": God's faithfulness toward us does not consist in delivering us from all temptation — for that would be to deprive Himself of His own glory, and to deprive us of the merit attached to the victory — but His faithfulness consists in never allowing the temptation to go beyond our strength for resisting.

God knows perfectly, and infinitely better than we do, what our strength really is, for we derive our strength solely from Him and His grace. He moderates the action of the tempter, for He always remains the supreme Master of that action; and He will never suffer the tempter to have more strength to attack than we have to resist.

This is not all: He will increase the power of His assistance in proportion to the strength of the temptation, so that we may be able to bear it and to come forth as conquerors. Thus

[29] 1 Cor. 10:13.

Do not be discouraged by temptations

He gives us more strength to resist than He allows the Devil to have to attack us. The greatness of the help increases in proportion to the violence of the temptation.

We fight, under the very eyes of God, and for Him, with the arms that He supplies to us, and we know by faith that it is never for want of His divine assistance, but always through our own fault, if we do not gain the victory. He wishes to punish us either for our past infidelities, or for our presumption, or for our want of confidence in Him. But if we give no occasion for our defeat, we are certain of victory through the help of God.

"But," you may say, "I do not feel this help." What does it matter whether you feel it or not, provided you really have it? God is only exercising your faith. While the Devil is stirring up tempests in your imagination, rousing all your passions, obscuring your understanding, shaking your will, and filling you with trouble, is it astonishing that you should not feel a help that is purely spiritual and that is acting only in the very depths of your soul?

"But I think I have consented. I am sure of it." Never judge that of yourself: God does not wish it. You will deceive yourself, and you will by this give the Devil power over you, and he will drive you to despair.

Rely in this entirely on the decision of your spiritual director, and humbly submit your own judgment to his. "What?" you will say. "In such a matter as this, on what passes in my innermost soul, on what has to do with my conscience and the salvation of my soul?" Yes. Your spiritual director has a light from God and sure rules to judge whether you have consented or not, and you have neither these rules nor this light to guide yourself. God wishes you to be guided by faith and obedience to die to your own judgment; He does not allow you to see clearly what is passing in the interior of your soul, above all in those terrible moments of trouble and darkness.

∞

Chapter Fourteen

Learn how to deal with your temptations

Having spoken of the usefulness and even the necessity of temptations, we must now say something about the manner in which we ought to act when temptations come.

Temptations differ according to the different states of the persons they attack; and this is something to which we must pay great attention, so that we may discern them well. The temptations of the generality of Christians lead them to evil under the appearance of some sensible good. These temptations are quite easy to recognize; and as they have nothing to do with persons who have given themselves entirely to God — the persons for whom I am specially writing — I shall say nothing about them, except that the only means of sheltering ourselves from this sort of temptation is to resolve most firmly to be attentive and faithful to divine grace even in the smallest matters, and to avoid not only mortal sin and all occasions that might lead us into it, but also venial sin and the slightest appearance of sin.

Whoever has generously decided on this course, and who faithfully pursues it, will no longer be exposed to this sort of temptation, which has no other root than the indecision of our will, as long as it is fluctuating between virtue and vice.

When we have given ourselves entirely and once and for all to God, He generally allows us to enjoy for some time a certain peace and tranquility of soul. He does not allow the Devil to trouble us, wishing to give us time to get up our strength and to put ourselves in a state to resist his attacks. But, as virtue has need of being tried, that thereby it may become confirmed, the temptations will come when God sees fit, or when the soul itself gives occasion for them by leaning too much on itself or reflecting too much on itself.

∾

The Devil tries to prevent us from doing good

The object of these temptations is, first, to withdraw us from a certain good through the fear of committing evil. For instance, the Devil will try to keep a soul away from Holy Communion through the fear of communicating unworthily or under pretense that the soul derives no profit from it. This fear is only a vague fear with which he troubles the imagination, and the only thing to do is to despise it and take no notice of it. This pretense comes only because we wish to judge the profit we derive from our Communions, which is what we ought never to do.

The second object of these temptations is to turn us away from doing good under pretense of loss of time and idleness. This happens above all with regard to prayer, when we have no longer good thoughts and affections, and when we are assailed with distractions. Then we immediately think we are doing nothing, and we are tempted to give up our way of prayer and return to ordinary meditation. This is a delusion that we must fight against strenuously. Prayer is the death of self-love, and it is never more effective for producing this death than when it is dry, distracted, and without any consolation or sensible devotion.

The third object of these temptations is to propose to us another way of doing good than that which God wills for us. For instance, God draws us to Himself by a love of retirement, of solitude, by a desire of enjoying His presence in peace and silence. And under pretense of zeal for souls, or charity, or edification to our neighbor, we allow ourselves to be drawn into all sorts of exterior good works and association with the outside world, and we even wish to undertake the conversion of souls to God. This is a temptation that is very frequent; and we must resist it by waiting until God Himself furnishes us with the occasion of serving our neighbor and shows us plainly that it is His will. We should never take the initiative of ourselves.

The Devil will also try to tempt us in the matter of obedience, either by giving us a bad impression of our director or by suggesting to us that he is deceived in our regard or that he goes beyond his authority. On this matter I have only one thing to say: once we have sufficient proof (and we always have it in the beginning) that our director is a good and upright man, that he is learned and enlightened, and that he is guided by the Spirit of God, we must obey him in all things as we would obey God Himself; we must never allow ourselves to judge him; and we must listen to nothing that might weaken our good opinion of him. Of course, I except those cases where there is palpable and notorious evidence of his having conducted himself badly; but such cases are very rare, and they are always easy to recognize.

The temptations of more advanced souls are quite of another order, and they are rather trials than temptations. God, who wishes to humble them, to purify them, and to annihilate self in them, allows the Devil to try them with violent temptations against purity, or against faith, hope, or love of God and neighbor. He allows a kind of universal upheaval or unchaining of the powers of evil. He may even allow exterior and apparent faults, to which the soul believes it has consented, although in reality it is very far from having done so.

It is, above all, in this kind of temptation that the guidance of an experienced and skillful spiritual director is absolutely necessary, and we have need of a perfect obedience of judgment and will; for the soul then is so troubled, the understanding is so obscured, that the soul is incapable of judging rightly on what is passing within itself, and it must absolutely rely on the judgment of another.

What the person must do then — and this is essential — is to hide nothing from his director, but to tell him faithfully and honestly, without fear or shame, and with great simplicity, exactly what he experiences. He must let him form his own judgment, without trying to influence him by his own, and without disputing with him. He must agree with his director's decision, without examination or reflection, and then do without hesitation whatever he may command, in spite of any fear he may have or any feeling that he has offended or is going to offend God.

Learn how to deal with your temptations

These states of the soul are very strange, undoubtedly, and the conscience suffers in them a terrible perplexity. But God allows them so that the soul may die completely to itself, to its own will, to its own interest. And the only way to pass through them safely is in a spirit of blind obedience, of perfect fidelity, and of entire resignation to the will of God.

∞

Learn how to respond to temptation

Besides what I have just said as to the manner in which we ought to behave during these different temptations, there are a few general rules to observe before, during, and after the temptations.

Before the temptation comes, we must neither fear it, nor even think of it, nor take any measure to anticipate it or to prevent it. I am speaking of the temptations of trial, in which the soul is entirely passive. We must simply keep ourselves, like little children, in the arms of God, placing in Him all our confidence and expecting everything from His help. The best preparation is an inviolable fidelity to divine grace and a generous courage in overcoming ourselves in all things, for the more we conquer nature, the less hold temptation has upon us; the Devil is strong against us only in proportion as we are weak through self-love.

During the immediate time of the temptation, we must let it pass over us like a stormy cloud, we must hold fast to God, and we must not give up any of our ordinary practices of devotion. Thus, even if we are assailed by the most horrible thoughts during the time of prayer, we must not leave off our prayer until the usual hour for doing so. Still less must we give up Holy Communion on the pretext of the impure or blasphemous thoughts that trouble us at that sacred moment. It is very often just this very time that the Devil chooses to torment us. Let us make a rule to ourselves never to yield to him, however hard he may press us.

"Resist the Devil," says St. James, "and he will flee from you."[30] He can do nothing against a soul that is firm and immovable; he must retire, overwhelmed with confusion. If our director has prescribed any particular practice during the time of temptation, we must be very faithful to it, because God always blesses obedience.

When the moment of temptation is over, we must enjoy the calm that is restored to our soul without examining whether we have consented or not: this could serve only to trouble and discourage us, for it is certain that it is not by the manner in which our soul is affected during the temptation that we can judge whether we have resisted or yielded. Our soul is then too much agitated to be able to discern what is free and what is not.

It is our general conduct after the temptation is over that alone can tell us of our victory or our defeat. If we are humble, docile, obedient, faithful in the observance of all our duties, and ready to renounce our own will, God will never allow us to be overcome, and it is upon this rule that the confessor must decide and reassure us, if he sees that it is right to do so. Therefore it is necessary for us to give him a faithful account of all we

[30] James 4:7.

have experienced, neither adding to nor diminishing any-thing, telling as certain what we believe to be certain, and as doubtful what we think doubtful. Everything else rests with the director.

What we ought, above all things, to forbid ourselves are reasonings and reflections on the temptation and its circum-stances. We ought never to think about it at all, except to speak of it to our director, and when that is done, we ought never willingly to let our mind dwell upon it at all.

∞

Chapter Fifteen

Trust God in all things

Of all the virtues, the most necessary is trust in God, because without it he can do nothing, and with it he can do everything. This virtue is the just medium between two extremes that are equally to be avoided, and into which, nevertheless, fall the greater part of men. Some fall into presumption, and others into cowardice. The first form to themselves a false idea of the goodness of God and abuse it either by offending Him or by relaxing their pursuit of perfection. "God," they say, "will never condemn me for such a little thing. He will give me time to do penance. He is not so exacting; He does not look into everything so closely."

The second class have a too lively fear of the justice of God and of the severity of His judgments. They scarcely ever think of His mercy. This fear freezes them, destroys their courage, and often throws them into despair.

Self-love and erroneous ideas are the source of these two extremes. We must keep the right middle course, which consists in so putting all our trust in God that we can never presume on His goodness, and also at the same time that we can never despair. It is only the souls that are truly devoted to God who know how to keep this just medium; all others deviate from it more or less. Men fall more easily into presumption, women into fear and mistrust.

∞

Trust in God is founded on
knowledge of Him and of ourselves

Trust in God is founded, on the one hand, on a right knowledge of God and on the other hand, on a right knowledge of ourselves. The knowledge of God teaches us that He is infinitely good in Himself, that He loves the creatures He has made, that He cannot help loving them and wishing well to them, and that their loss, if they are lost, can never be His doing. Religion teaches us that He loves us incomparably more than it is possible to imagine or conceive. He loves us to such a degree that He gave up His own Son and delivered Him to death for us. He presents us with His grace. He is always ready to receive the sinner who returns to Him. He will pardon the sinner and forget all his faults, provided only that he sincerely repents; and He never ceases to follow the sinner, in all his wanderings, in order to bring him back to Himself.

If we will only enter a little into ourselves, and reflect on the course of our life, experience will teach us that, in all, God has behaved toward us with a mercy that is infinite, that He has preserved some of us from sin and has withdrawn us from the occasions of it; that He has for a long time borne with the constant falls of others of us; that He could have damned us after our first mortal sin, and that He did not do so; that He has contrived all kinds of assistance to help us to return to Him; and that it is to Him alone that we owe our escape from the power of sin or our perseverance in doing good. Let us bring back to our memory all the personal graces we have received from Him, and besides those we know of, let us be quite sure that there are many, many others that we are either ignorant of or have forgotten. How many motives may we draw from all this to place all our trust in God!

And the motives drawn from the knowledge of ourselves are not less important. I can do nothing — absolutely nothing — of myself, in the spiritual life. Not only am I weak, but my strength is nothing at all. I can make a bad use of my free will; I can ruin myself forever, if I choose; but my free will, without God's grace, cannot save me. I cannot save myself. I need the help of an ever-present grace, and this help is granted only to an earnest prayer that is inspired by a perfect trust in God. If I fall, it is impossible for me to rise again unless God stretches out His hand to me, and He will stretch it out to me as soon as I call upon Him. I can never rely on my own promises, or my good impulses, or my good resolutions; experience has proven this to me a thousand times. As to the dangers and temptations that surround the path of virtue, it would be the greatest blindness on my part to think I could protect myself against them by my own strength.

In short, the whole work of my salvation, from the beginning to the end, depends on God alone. He has in His hands the infallible means of bringing it to pass; and in spite of all my weaknesses and my misery, and my inclination to evil, He will most assuredly bring about my salvation if I never lose my confidence in Him, if I expect everything from His mercy, if I keep myself always united to Him. It is, therefore, quite true that the more humility we have — that is to say, the better we know ourselves — the more trust we have in God.

Now, a trust that is based on humility can never be presumptuous. And, on the other hand, a trust that has for its basis the infinite goodness of God, His great love for His creatures, and His great power — such a trust can never be timid and cowardly. For what can he fear who finds all his support in God? "Throw yourself into His arms," says St. Augustine. "He will not take them away; He will not let you fall." And when once we are in the arms of God, what enemy can harm us? What temptation can tear us away from Him?

∞

Have a proper fear of God's justice

"But the justice of God is very terrible," you may say, "and I ought always to fear it." That is quite true. But for whom is His justice terrible? Is it for those children of God who love Him and serve Him as a Father, who are determined to refuse Him nothing and to displease Him in nothing? No. If these children love God, God loves them still more; He sees that their faults are not faults of malice but of imperfection and human weakness. At the first look of love and sorrow that they turn to Him, He will forgive them; and even if He has to punish them, He will punish them in this world, in the way that is most advantageous for their salvation.

Is it for the sinners who return to God sincerely that His justice is terrible? No. They experience the effects of His great mercy; and often they are treated with so much tenderness and love that even the just are jealous of them. We have only to think of Mary Magdalene and of the Prodigal Son.[31]

The Divine Justice is terrible only for those who will not have recourse to His mercy, either through presumption or through despair; for those who love sin and do not wish to give it up; for those whose will is not straightforward and upright, and who would like, if they could, to deceive God Himself.

But it is quite clear that such sinners as these have not and cannot have any real trust in God; it is clear that they have no right to this trust; for real trust in God can begin only from the time that we begin sincerely to desire to renounce sin and to be overcome with shame and sorrow at having offended God.

God wishes us to fear His justice, so that we may avoid sin, so that we may forsake it as soon as possible, so that we may expiate it by penance, so that we may never think we have expiated it sufficiently, and so that we may not lightly presume on the hope of pardon. But at the same time He wishes us to trust in Him, to hope for all things from His mercy, to return to Him through love rather than fear, and never to allow ourselves to become the prey of a terror that is without foundation and injurious to God, and that can have no other effect than to discourage and dishearten us.

But how far are we to carry this trust in God? As far as His power and His goodness; as far as our own weakness and our own misery; that is to say, our trust is to be boundless.

[31] Cf. Luke 7:36-50; 15:11-32.

Thus, however difficult perfection may be, we must strive after it with humility and confidence, without being frightened at the difficulties and dangers in the way. But, as, when we consider ourselves, we ought always to say, "I can do nothing," so when we consider God, who will be our Guide and Support on the way, we ought to say, "I can do all things through Him, and by His grace I shall succeed."

∞
Do not fear the world

But the world is very much to be feared. "Have confidence," said our Lord and Master, Jesus Christ. "I have overcome the world."[32] He overcame it in His own Person; He will overcome it again in ours. Is the world more formidable for us than it was for so many martyrs and so many saints? Had these martyrs and saints any strength of themselves? Not any more than we have; but they were strong with the strength of God, and we can be so, as they were.

But the snares of the Devil are so crafty and so powerful. The Devil can do nothing against a humble trust in God. Never presume on your own strength; expect everything from God, and all the powers of Hell will never be able to hurt you.

But self-love corrupts everything, poisons everything; it is always to be feared, whatever progress we may have made. Always, then, distrust yourself; be always on your guard against your own judgment and your own will. Increase each day in the love of God, and each day you will weaken self-love.

[32] John 16:33.

Sacrifice all your own interests to those of God; leave to Him the care of all that concerns you, and occupy yourself only with doing His will. Do not refer God to yourself, but refer yourself to God for everything that is of any consequence to you, in time and in eternity, and self-love will be lost in the love of God.

But we must pass through many trials and humiliations to die entirely to ourselves. Yes, and this goes much farther than you can possibly imagine or foresee. But the more generously you accept these trials and humiliations, the more God will support you. Your courage and strength will increase beyond measure; or rather, in proportion as you lose your own strength, you will acquire the strength of God, and with that you will become capable of everything, superior to everything. And your victory over the world, over the Devil, and over yourself will be the effect of your trust in God. "Perfect love," St. John says, "casts out fear"[33] — all fear, except the fear of offending God or of refusing Him anything.

[33] 1 John 4:18.

Chapter Sixteen

∞

Maintain interior peace

Fly; keep silence; rest: These three words, which were spoken by a voice from Heaven to St. Arsenius,[34] contain everything that it is necessary for us to do on our part to correspond with the designs of God for us.

We must fly from all that could draw us away from God; we must keep ourselves in a silence both exterior and interior, so that we may hear the voice of God; and we must calm all the agitations and anxieties of our mind and heart, so that they may be fixed on God alone.

∞

Free yourself from worldly things

All souls whom God destines for the interior life are not called, as St. Arsenius was, to fly from the world and to retire into complete solitude, but all are called to use this world as though they used it not, to detach from it their mind and heart, and to have with it only those relations which are

---

[34] St. Arsenius (d. c. 450), confessor and hermit in Egypt.

indispensable; in short, in all their dealings with the world, to avoid everything that could separate them from God.

Now, this detachment goes much farther and is much more difficult than appears at first sight. It is not sufficient to avoid everything that is actual sin or that leads to actual sin. We must also avoid all that pleases our senses, curiosity, esteem of ourselves, and the desire of being praised, approved, or thought much of; all that is capable of distracting us, of drawing our soul toward external things, and taking it out of itself and of that peaceful center where God deigns to dwell. We cannot be too careful in this matter, because our exterior relations with the world are one of the principal sources of our faults and the most ordinary cause of our slight progress in the spiritual life.

That which makes the great difficulty of this perfect detachment is the powerful inclination in our soul to pour itself out upon created things, to allow them to lead it astray, to seek in them its repose, and to attribute to them a reality and a solidity that they do not have. This is the sad effect of Original Sin, even in the most innocent souls, but much more so in those who have had the misfortune to have actually offended God.

The next great difficulty comes from the love we have for ourselves and the desire we have to be loved and esteemed by others. If we wish people to love us, we must love them and love what they love. If we wish to be esteemed by them, we must esteem them; we must think, we must speak, we must act as they do. This is a law that the world imposes upon us — a law that self-love persuades us to be a duty and to which are sacrificed often the laws of God, the maxims of the Gospel, and the light of reason and conscience.

If we associate with the world other than through necessity and absolute charity, and even then fortifying ourselves interiorly against its seductions, it is quite impossible for us not to end by conforming to its judgments and opinions, and to its natural, human, and sensual ideas. We do this either to please others, or from human respect, or from being carried away, almost without our consent. It is quite impossible for us not to end by approving or at least excusing in others those things which God expressly condemns, because we are afraid of making ourselves ridiculous if we think differently from other people and if we dare to oppose the pure maxims of the gospel to the maxims received by the world.

What must we do, then, to practice this flight from the world, which is so necessary and so recommended to us? We must look on the world as the greatest enemy to the Christian Faith, and as the most dangerous deceiver, because it always agrees but too well with the promptings of our own self-love.

We must retire from the world as much as possible; we must break with all useless ties that have no other object than amusement. We must speak but little in company and not always say what we wish to say; but when we are obliged to speak, we must do so plainly and without human respect, remembering those words of our Lord Jesus Christ: "Whoever shall be ashamed of me before men, of him will I be ashamed before my Father in Heaven."[35]

[35] Cf. Mark 8:38.

The Spiritual Life

∞

Maintain a certain silence

We must keep silence, both exteriorly and interiorly. It is a great mistake to imagine that the practice of silence is only for those souls consecrated to God in the life of the cloister. It is necessary for everyone who wishes to lead a really interior life; and it was not for religious alone that Jesus Christ said that on the day of judgment we must give an account of every idle word.[36]

Great freedom of speech is the sure mark of a frivolous and dissipated soul. I defy anyone to come away from a useless conversation and to return easily to a state of recollection, or to prayer or spiritual reading, with the peace and calm that are necessary for drawing any profit from such devout exercises.

But it is not enough to keep silence with others. We must keep silence with ourselves: we must not indulge our imagination; we must not be always thinking of what we have said or heard; we must not occupy ourselves with useless thoughts and reflections on the past and the future. How can God make His voice heard by a soul so dissipated? And if the soul allows itself thus to roam over all sorts of objects, how can it recollect itself for prayer? It is not a little thing to be able to master our imagination, to control it, to fix it on the present, on what we are actually doing, and not to allow it to pause willingly before that crowd of thoughts that pass continually through our minds.

I know that we cannot help having these kind of thoughts; but we can help letting our heart dwell on them; we can

[36] Matt. 12:36.

124

despise them and take no notice of them. When such thoughts come from some trouble, from some revolt of self-love, or from some inordinate desire, we can make a sacrifice to God of that trouble, subdue that revolt, or repress that desire. The exercise of interior mortification is an efficacious means, and more than that, it is the only means by which we can attain that perfect silence of the soul which disposes us for close communion with God.

∞

Let God guide your soul

Finally, we must commend to God the agitations and anxieties of our mind and heart. It is in vain that we seek for rest outside of God; we can find it only in God, and in God alone. It is not by agitating ourselves, by being very eager and doing many external acts, that we succeed in resting in God; it is when we give up all agitation, all eagerness, all activity, and allow God to act on us.

God is always in action and yet always at rest. And the soul that is closely united to Him shares in His action and in His rest. That soul is always in action, even when it does not perceive it; but it acts always in the greatest peace. It does not forerun the action of God, but waits for Him to direct it; it moves under the divine guidance, like the hand of a child who is learning to write moves under the guidance of his master's hand. If this child did not keep his hand supple and docile, if he wished to form the letters by himself, he would write badly. The child does undoubtedly act in writing, but his action is directed by the action of his master. The repose of the child does not consist in not moving his hand, but in not moving it of himself, and in simply following the guidance of the guiding hand.

So it is with the faithful soul under the immediate action of God: the soul is not idle for a moment, as those imagine who have no idea of what true rest in God means. God guides the rudder of that soul and leads it as He will. It is quite true that the action of God on the soul, as well as the action of the soul itself, is sometimes imperceptible, but it is nonetheless real: only then it is even more direct, closer, more spiritual.

Even in a natural state, how many interior movements are there of which we take no note, which are nevertheless the motive-principle of our exterior actions? I look, I speak, I walk, I turn away my eyes, I keep silence, I stop, just because I will to do so; and, in a general way, I pay no attention to this constant exercise of my will. It is just the same, and still more so, in the supernatural state. We pray without thinking that we are praying; our heart is united to God, and we are not conscious of this union.

Therefore, it must not be said that those whom God raises to this prayer of quiet are doing nothing and losing their time: they are in reality acting there in a manner that is very real, although very secret, and, besides that, in a manner in which self-love can find nothing to nourish it, or to attract it, or to reassure it. And it is in this that the great advantage of this state of prayer consists; it is the very death and destruction of self-love; it is the soul losing itself entirely in God. As long as the soul thinks itself conscious of its state, as long as it knows where it is and how it stands, it is not lost; it has still something to lean on.

When does the soul begin to be lost in God? It is when it feels nothing anymore, when it no longer sees anything in itself, when it has ceased to look within, and when, ceasing to reason or reflect upon itself, it abandons itself entirely to the guidance of God. God will lead that soul by degrees in this way of loss. He will guide it by this prayer which has nothing sensible, until at last, because the soul finds no resource, either in itself or in any man, its trust is established in God alone, and, like Jesus Christ on the Cross, forsaken by all men, and apparently by His Father also, that soul can say, "Father, into Thy hands I commend my spirit."[37] I give myself to Thee, to do as Thou wilt with me, in time and in eternity.

It is to this great act of resignation, so glorious to God and so useful to the soul, that the prayer of quiet leads, when it is well understood and rightly practiced. Of ourselves we cannot enter upon this way of prayer; of ourselves we cannot advance in it; but when God has raised us to it, we must have the courage to follow it and to persevere to the end. This grace is given to very few souls. And St. Teresa complains that so many give up the prayer of quiet and go no farther when their prayer ceases to be sensible and perceptible — that is to say, just when it begins to be most profitable to the soul, through the mortification of self-love.

Let us not be of the number of those cowardly souls who seek only themselves in the service of God; let us seek Him for Himself alone, and most surely we shall find Him, and in Him the source of all good.

[37] Luke 23:46.

Chapter Seventeen

Be faithful to God in little things

Holy Scripture has said two things that may convince us of the importance of faithfulness in little things: "He that despises small things," we are told, "shall fall by little and little."[38]

And our Lord Jesus Christ said, "He that is faithful in that which is least shall be faithful also in that which is greater."[39]

We see from the first passage that the neglect of little things exposes us infallibly to great falls; and from the second, that fidelity in little things ensures our fidelity in great things and is consequently a necessary means of mortification. We need only to understand these two thoughts well to be inviolably faithful on the smallest occasion.

To develop this matter a little more, let us remark, in the first place, that, properly speaking, there is nothing either little or great with regard to the things of God. Everything that bears the impress of His will is great, however small it may be in itself. Thus, as soon as we are quite sure, by an interior

---

[38] Ecclus. 19:1 (RSV = Sir. 19:1).
[39] Luke 16:10.

voice, that God desires some particular thing of us, the infinite greatness of God does not allow us to regard as small or indifferent that thing which is the object of His desire. On the contrary, however great in itself a thing may be, were it even the conversion of the whole world, if God does not require it from us, any idea of the kind that we might form to ourselves would have no value in His eyes and might even displease Him. It is only the will of God that gives any value to things.

In the same way, with regard to our sanctification, such and such a thing, which appears to us very little in itself, may be of so great consequence that our perfection, and even our salvation, may depend on it. God attaches His grace to what pleases Him. We cannot know of ourselves what may be the good or evil consequences of any single action that seems to us of little importance. Of what grace may I be deprived if I neglect it? What grace may come to me if I perform it? This is just what I do not know; in this uncertainty a constant and exact fidelity to grace is the only course to pursue.

∞

Faithfulness in little things
gives us courage to do great things

Now, great things and great occasions of heroic virtue are rarely presented to us. But little things are offered to us every day. And how shall we ever prove our love to God if we wait for grand and brilliant occasions? Perhaps one may never come to us all our life long.

More than this, great things require great courage. How can we make sure of our strength in heroic actions if we have made no trial of it in small ones; if we have not striven and prepared ourselves by degrees for difficult things by the performance of those that are easier?

Great things, also, cannot be accomplished without great graces on the part of God. But to merit and obtain these great and special graces, we must have been faithful to the smaller graces. Humility wishes that we look on great things as far above us and that we never of ourselves aspire to them; humility teaches us to attach ourselves to little things, as being more within our reach. Let us, then, perform our little and everyday actions with fidelity to our ordinary graces, and let us be quite sure that, when God requires greater things from us, He will certainly care to give us the necessary graces.

The desire of doing and suffering great things is often — indeed almost always — an illusion of self-love and an effect of presumption. I would like to practice great austerities; like such and such a saint, I would like to bear great crosses: this is all pride, all vainglory.

The saints never formed such desires. Now, what happens to us when we do? We try of our own will to perform great austerities; then our fervor cools down, and we give them up; then some very ordinary crosses present themselves to us, and our soul, which thought it could bear such great things, finds it cannot bear the very smallest.

Let us desire nothing; let us choose nothing; let us take things just as God sends them to us and just when He chooses to send them to us; let us think nothing of our own courage and strength, but believe ourselves inferior to the weakest; and let us be persuaded that if God did not take pity on our weakness and did not sustain us by His strength, we could not advance a single step.

And, as little things are constantly recurring, an exact fidelity to them requires more courage, more generosity, and more constancy than we would think at first sight. To do it perfectly requires nothing less than consummate virtue; for, indeed, it is a question of dying to ourselves at every moment, of following in all things the guidance of divine grace, of never allowing ourselves a thought, or desire, or word, or action that could give the least displeasure to God, and of doing everything, even to the simplest thing, with the perfection He requires of us; and all this without any relaxation, without ever granting anything to nature. In very truth, we must confess that in all sanctity there is nothing greater than this constant fidelity, nothing that needs a more sustained effort.

∞

Faithfulness in little things fosters humility
There is much danger of self-love being mixed up with the great things that we do or suffer for God. There is much danger of our applauding our own courage, taking credit for it, or preferring ourselves to others. Little things do not expose us to the same danger; it is easier in them to preserve humility; in them there is nothing for self-love to fix on as matter for glorification; there is no occasion for comparing ourselves with others and preferring ourselves to them.

Therefore, the faithful practice of little things is incomparably safer for us and far more conducive to our perfection, which consists in dying entirely to ourselves. Little things

destroy and consume by degrees our self-love, almost without
its perceiving the blows directed against it. These blows are
slight; but they are so frequent and so varied that they have as
much effect as the most violent blows.

And even if the death of self-love is more gradual, it is
nonetheless sure, for the constant practice of little things reduces it to such a state of weakness that at last it has no power
of reviving. Therefore, it is generally in this way that God fin-
ishes our self-love. Sometimes, in the beginning, He may deal
it great blows; but it is by these quiet and scarcely perceptible
blows that He reduces it to the last extremity. The soul then
no longer knows what to do; God seems to take away everything from it and to leave it naked and destitute. The soul no
longer takes pleasure in anything; it seems scarcely to be doing
anything; it remains in a kind of annihilation, in which God
acts so greatly within it that it perceives neither the action of
God nor its own.

∞

Faithfulness in little things
proves our love for God

If the love of God seems to shine with more generosity in
great sacrifices, it shows in little sacrifices, continually re-
peated, more attention and more delicacy. We do not love
perfectly when we neglect small occasions of pleasing the one
whom we love and when we do not fear to wound him by trifles. The jealousy of God is infinite; it extends to everything; it
embraces everything; and if human love is so exacting, so all-
absorbing, divine love is infinitely more so. And every soul

who truly loves will try never to give this divine jealousy any cause of offense. To wound the tender and loving Heart of God in the least thing will be for that soul a crime that will inspire it with the greatest horror. And to refuse anything whatever to God, deliberately and intentionally, under the pretext that it is nothing, is to fail in love in a most essential particular; it is to renounce our familiarity with God, our close union with Him; it is to deprive Him of His greatest glory. For it is in this that He makes His glory to consist — that is, that His creature shall never look upon anything as small that can please or displease Him, and that His creature shall always be disposed to sacrifice everything to His good pleasure. It is quite certain that we do not begin to love God with a love that is really worthy of Him until we have entered into these dispositions.

I am not speaking here of our own interest. But it is easy to see that a soul that is faithful to its resolution of pleasing God in the smallest things will most assuredly gain the Heart of God; that it will draw to itself all His tenderness, all His favors, all His graces; that by such a practice it will amass at every moment inconceivable treasures of merit; and that, in the end, it will be capable of doing for God the greatest things, if He should call it to perform them.

These are, it seems to me, quite sufficient motives to make us take at once the great and heroic determination to neglect nothing in the service of God, but to apply ourselves to please Him in everything, without distinction of great or small. Let us, then, make this determination once for all; and let us beg God that we may be faithful to it until our last breath.

Be faithful to God in little things

Nevertheless, we must take care to carry our resolution into execution without too much care or anxiety. Love wishes for a holy liberty; everything consists in never losing sight of God, and in doing from one moment to another just what His grace inspires us to do, and in turning away at once from anything that we know would displease Him. He will never fail to give us warnings in the interior of our souls whenever we need them. And when He does not give us such warnings, we may rest assured that there is nothing in what we have said or done that was contrary to His good pleasure. And if we do not allow anything to draw us from our recollection in Him, we cannot fail to know whether we have received any interior warning or not, and whether we have followed it. Thus, there is never the least occasion for us to torment ourselves unnecessarily.

Chapter Eighteen

∞

Let your soul rest in God

"Come unto me, all you that labor and are burdened, and I will refresh you: and you shall find rest for your souls."[40] This invitation was addressed to every man on earth. No one other than Jesus Christ has ever given them such an invitation; and they have all the greatest interest in experiencing the reality of this promise.

We all suffer in this world more or less, either from anxiety of mind, or sorrow of heart, or pain of body. And nevertheless we all long for rest; we seek it eagerly; and we wear ourselves out all our lives in this search without ever attaining the object of our desires.

Where is rest to be found? Where shall we seek it? This is a most interesting question if ever there was one.

Some men, in fact the greater number, seek their rest in the enjoyment of the riches, pleasures, and honors of this life. What care do they not take to secure these things for themselves, to preserve them, to increase them, and to accumulate them?

[40] Matt. 11:28, 29.

The Spiritual Life

Do they really find rest in these things? No. How would rest be found in these perishing things, which cannot even satisfy the passion that desired them; in things that have no proportion with the wants of the human heart, that leave it always empty, always devoured by a still more ardent thirst; in things that are always being disputed and envied and torn furiously by one person from another? What rest and stability can be found in things that are change itself? If the foundation on which we build our rest is always moving, is it not a necessary consequence that we must experience the same agitation?

Let everyone consult himself; experience is the most positive of proofs. What man ever tasted rest in the midst of the greatest treasures, the liveliest pleasures, the most flattering honors? Rest is not in these things: everyone knows this; and yet it is in these things that man persists in seeking it. Men exhaust themselves in desires, in projects, in enterprises, and they never succeed in finding a single moment of rest. If they would only consult their reason, it would tell them that in this way they can never find rest. What blindness! What folly!

Others establish their rest in themselves, and in doing this, they think they are much wiser than those who seek it in exterior things. But are they really wise? Is man made to be sufficient for himself? Can he find in himself the principle of his rest? His ideas change every day; his heart is in a perpetual state of unrest; he is constantly imagining new systems of happiness, and he finds this happiness nowhere. If he is alone, he is devoured with weariness. If he is in company, however select and agreeable it may be, it soon becomes tiresome to him; his reflections exhaust and torment him. Study and reading may amuse him and distract him for a time, but they cannot fill up the void in his heart. This is the kind of rest that human wisdom promises to its followers and for which it invites them to give up everything else, to isolate themselves, and to concentrate their attention on themselves. It is a deceitful rest, which is not exempt from the most violent agitations and which is at least as hard for man to bear as the tumult of his passions!

Where, then, is rest to be found, if we can find it neither in the good things of this world nor in ourselves?

It is to be found in God, and in God alone. Jesus Christ came into the world to teach us this truth, and it is the greatest lesson that He has given us. But how few there are who profit by it!

"Thou hast made us for Thyself," cries St. Augustine, "and our heart finds no rest until it reposes in Thee." This truth is the first principle of all morality; reason, religion, and experience all unite in proving it to us.

∞

Resting in God requires abandoning ourselves to Him

But to repose in God, what must we do? We must give ourselves entirely to Him, and we must sacrifice to Him everything else. If we give ourselves only partly to Him, if we make some reservation, if we keep back some attachment, it is quite clear that our rest cannot be entire or perfect, because trouble will glide in by the place in our heart that is not united to God and resting only on Him. This is why so few Christians enjoy a real peace — a peace that is continual, full, and unchanging.

The Spiritual Life

They do not fix their rest in God alone; they do not entrust everything to Him; they do not abandon everything to Him. Nevertheless, there is no true and solid rest to be found but in this utter abandonment.

This rest is unchangeable, as God is. It is elevated, as God is, above all created things. It is most secret and intimate, because it is only God, the enjoyment of whom pierces to the very depths of our hearts. It is full, because God completely fills and satisfies the heart. It leaves nothing to desire and nothing to regret, because he who possesses God can neither desire nor regret anything else. This rest calms the passions, tranquilizes the imagination, composes the mind, and fixes the inconstancy of the heart. This rest subsists in the midst of all changes of fortune of every imaginable evil and misfortune, even in the midst of temptations and trials, because nothing in these things can reach the center of the soul that is reposing in God.

The martyrs on the scaffold, a prey to the most horrible tortures, the confessors, in poverty, in prison, in exile, in persecution, tasted this rest in the depths of their souls, and were happy. The saints have tasted it in solitude, in the exercise of a most austere penance, in hard and excessive labors, in calumnies, in humiliations, in infirmities and sicknesses. A crowd of Christians have tasted it in the painful duties of their state of life, in the crosses attached to it, in the common life and all the cares and anxieties it entails.

It depends only on ourselves to enjoy it as they did. If we will it, God will be to us what He has been to them. He asks of us, as He asked of them, only a single thing: that we should lean only on Him and seek our rest and happiness in Him alone.

The experience of this is certain and has never failed. From the moment that we give our hearts to God, that we put our conscience in order, that we take measures to avoid all sin — venial as well as mortal — that we make a firm determination to be attentive and faithful to divine grace, and to refuse nothing to God, that we put ourselves under the direction of an enlightened guide and resolve to obey him in all things — from that moment, we enter upon a rest and a peace that we have never before experienced, of which we could have formed no idea, and at which we are utterly astonished.

∞

Resting in God brings us peace

This rest is at first very sweet and pleasant. We enjoy it, and we feel that we are enjoying it; it draws us and concentrates us within ourselves. When we have this rest, nothing troubles us; nothing wearies us. Any position, however painful it would otherwise be, is agreeable to us. All other pleasures, whatever they may be, become tasteless and insipid to us. We avoid carefully everything that could withdraw us from this sweet enjoyment of the peace of God. No miser ever feared so much to lose his treasure as we fear everything that could take away from us our rest or change it in any way. This is that blessed sleep of the soul, in which it wakes for God alone and sleeps for everything else.

This may seem like a dream, a fancy, or an illusion to those who have never experienced it. And it is not only worldlings who think thus; all those to whom rest is unknown, because they have not really given themselves to God, treat it as a delusion or as the wandering of an overheated imagination.

But let us rather believe the saints, who speak of it from their own experience. Let us believe St. Paul, who speaks to us of the "peace that passes all understanding."[41] Let us believe our Lord Jesus Christ, who calls this rest His peace, a divine peace, which the world can neither give nor take away[42] — a peace that we can never obtain by our own efforts because it is the gift of God and is His reward for the absolute and irrevocable gift of ourselves that we have made to Him.

I have said before that this peace has its trials and often even very severe trials; but far from shaking it, these trials only strengthen it. This peace of God rises above all evils and raises us with it. It renders a Christian so happy in the midst of all his sufferings that he would not change his state, however terrible it may seem to human nature, for the most exquisite pleasures the world could offer him. Such is the life of a perfect Christian who goes to God by Jesus Christ and who adores God as Christ adored Him, in spirit and in truth; who sacrifices everything to God, and himself above all. Nothing can destroy the rest and peace of his soul, and death will be for him only a short passage from his rest in time to his eternal rest.

[41] Phil. 4:7.
[42] Cf. John 14:27.

∞

Chapter Nineteen

Let the crucifix remind you of God's love

St. Paul said that all religion was contained for him in the science of the crucifix — "Jesus Christ, and Him crucified"[43] — and most assuredly he was right. The crucifix is the abridgment of all that a Christian ought to believe and all that he ought to practice. The crucifix makes known to us all the malice of sin, the excess of our misery, and the still greater excess of divine love and mercy. The crucifix is the greatest proof that God — God as He is — could give us of His love, and it is the strongest motive He could employ to gain our hearts in return. Every virtue is included in the crucifix, and it is the consummation of the way of perfection. I will say a few words on each of these subjects, but grace will say many more to devout souls who wish to devote themselves entirely to the love of God.

The crucifix is the abridgment of all that a Christian ought to believe. The Divine Person who suffers there, the only Son of God, conceived in the womb of Mary by the operation of

---

[43] 1 Cor. 2:2.

the Holy Spirit, proposes to us the two great mysteries of the Trinity and the Incarnation. The object of His sufferings teaches us the mysteries of the Redemption and of Original Sin. The mystery of predestination, the mystery of grace, and the will of God to save all men are also contained in the crucifix. It is the source of all the sacraments; and all the worship by which the Church honors God springs from the Sacrifice of the Cross.

∞

The crucifix illustrates Christian living

The crucifix is the abridgment of all that a Christian ought to practice. All the morality of the Gospel consists in bearing our cross, in renouncing ourselves, in crucifying our flesh with all its corrupt affections and inclinations, and in sacrificing ourselves to the will of God. Jesus Christ has prescribed no law and has given no counsel that does not find its perfect accomplishment and its perfect model in the Cross. It is the most striking and living expression of the whole teaching of the Gospel.

∞

The crucifix reveals the malice of sin

The crucifix makes known to us all the malice of sin. What greater evil can there be, indeed, than that which caused the death of God-made-man? Before Jesus Christ came, it was possible to form some idea of what it was to offend God, but it was a very feeble and imperfect idea. The eternal punishment of Hell, although it goes beyond all created intelligence, is not even sufficient for the malice of sin, because it can punish sin but cannot expiate it. It required nothing less than a Divine Person to atone worthily, by His sufferings and humiliations, for the injury done to God by the sin of man. Therefore, it is at the foot of the Cross that we learn what sin really is and learn to feel all the horror of it that it deserves.

∞

The crucifix shows us our own misery
The crucifix makes known to us also the excess of our misery, an excess so great that it was impossible for us to remedy it of ourselves. The whole human race would have been lost, lost without hope, lost for all eternity, deprived forever of the possession of the Sovereign Good, if Jesus Christ by His death had not redeemed it, reconciled it with God, and re-established it in its rights and its hopes. Original Sin alone is enough to condemn us; but how many actual sins, incomparably more grievous, have we not added to that! Into what an abyss of misery have we not willfully plunged ourselves!

∞

The crucifix reveals divine love and mercy
But the crucifix makes known to us at the same time the still greater excess of the divine love and mercy. One abyss has attracted another abyss; the abyss of our misery has been absorbed and swallowed up in the infinite abyss of God's mercy. Oh, what reason David had to say that the mercies of God are above all His works! All that God has done in the order of nature is nothing compared with what He has done in the order

of grace. The goodness of the All-Powerful has infinitely surpassed itself in the work of our redemption. Never, even in Heaven, will our understanding rise to the full comprehension of the greatness of this benefit that faith places before our eyes when we look at our crucifix.

God, all God as He is, could not possibly have given us a greater proof of His love. Whatever proof He wished to give us of His love, it must have accorded with all the rights of His justice, which He could not give up. It was necessary that this justice should be appeased — but by whom? Who could possibly satisfy it, avenge it, and at the same time, spare the guilty?

Oh, admirable invention of divine love! God lays upon His own Son all our iniquities; He punishes them in His Person; He revenges Himself upon Him. And this adorable Son consents with all His heart to be for us the Victim of His Father's anger. What a love in the Father! What a love in the Son! Who can think of it without being ravished with astonishment and admiration, and penetrated with gratitude? If God had left to us the choice of a remedy for our evil case, would we ever have imagined such a remedy as this? And even if it had presented itself to our minds, would we ever have dared to propose it? Such a way of salvation could have been conceived only in the heart of a God who loved us infinitely.

And if our hearts can resist so much love, what hardness on our part! What malice! What ingratitude!

God strikes His own Son to deliver us from Hell and to open to us the gates of Paradise. He exhausts His anger upon His Son and forgives us. He adopts us as His own children in this divine Son. He gives us a right to share in His Son's inheritance, and He showers on us all the supernatural help we need to attain it. And what does He ask of us in return? That we should love Him, that we should serve Him, and that we should obey Him.

And we do not love Him! And we look on His service as an insupportable yoke! And we violate all His commandments! And all these crimes, all these scandals reign today, in the midst of a people calling themselves Christians, with as much or even more license than they did among the heathen of old! And irreligion is carried to such a degree that Jesus Christ and His Cross have become an object of contempt, and of mockery, and of horror! The very incomprehensibility and mystery of this love of God is precisely the reason for which it is rejected.

Is it possible to conceive such an excess of impiety? Is it possible to conceive how much this love of God, which is despised, insulted, and outraged, must be irritated against all these so-called Christians, who are really apostates, either secret or declared?

Ah, what a powerful motive this is for good and holy souls to love God with their whole heart and to try to atone, by their devotion, for so many outrages.

∞

The crucifix teaches virtue

And what virtue is there of which the crucifix is not the perfect model? Love of God, trust in God, resignation to the will of God, even when it seems most severe — an invariable patience, charity for others, forgiveness of injuries, love of enemies, humility, poverty, utter self-renunciation — and all these virtues carried to the greatest height of perfection, exercised under the most trying circumstances, and practiced with a courage and generosity worthy of God-made-man. Shall we complain, after all this, of what virtue costs us? Shall we argue with God about trifles? Shall we dare to reproach Him with requiring too much from us?

One look at our crucifix will make us blush for our complaints and our cowardice. What have we ever suffered, what can we ever suffer, for our salvation, that approaches ever so little to the sufferings and humiliations of Jesus Christ for us?

"But," you may say, "He was God, and I am only a weak creature." Certainly He was God; that is quite true, and therefore He suffered everything that it was possible for a human nature united to the divine nature to suffer. If the hypostatic union[44] communicated to His sacred humanity a strength infinite in the Giver, it was only that He might suffer in proportion; and the justice of God loaded His sacred humanity unsparingly with the greatest weight it could possibly bear. It is an article of Faith that God will never permit us to be tried beyond our strength.

Weak as we are, we can always bear the trials He sends us, because the measure of strength He gives us also equals and surpasses the measure of our sorrows. Thus, it is wrong for us to complain of our weakness and to think that the example of our Savior is not for us.

[44] That is, the union of the divine and human natures in the person of Jesus Christ.

Let the crucifix remind you of God's love

∾

The crucifix shows us the way of perfection

Finally, the crucifix is the consummation of the way of perfection. It shows us Jesus Christ as a Priest and a Victim at the same time — Jesus sacrificing Himself for the glory of His Father, sacrificing Himself willingly, and devoting Himself to the justice of God. There are but a very few favored souls whom God calls to this state of victim and this exact resemblance to Jesus crucified. But those who have reason to believe that God has called them to this honor must take their part in the sufferings and humiliations of their Savior; they must plant His Cross in their hearts, or rather, they must let Him plant it and bury it there. Jesus, submissive and obedient even unto death, must be their model, their consolation, and their strength. And if sometimes their sufferings seem to them excessive, if their courage begins to fail, if they are tempted to accuse God of an unjust severity, let them fix their eyes on the crucifix. Jesus on the Cross will be an answer to everything, and they will leave His presence with the desire to suffer more.

∾

Learn from the crucifix

Let the crucifix, then, be our chief spiritual book. Let it be a book, not for our eyes only, but for our hearts! Let us beg Jesus to teach us how to read in it and to reveal to us all its secrets, not only so that we may contemplate them in the sweetness of prayer, but so that we may practice them faithfully during the whole course of our life. Let us enter upon the way of perfection with an absolute and unreserved devotion to the will of

God. Let us resign our souls entirely to the workings of His Spirit and His grace. Let us make with a generous heart every sacrifice that He asks of us; and let us beg Him to take from us and forcibly tear from us all that we have not the courage to give Him of ourselves.

In a word, let us try to reduce ourselves to the state of Jesus Christ dying on the Cross, in agony, with the scorn of men, forsaken apparently by His Father, uniting in His soul and body all the imaginable sufferings of a Victim to the Divine Justice and to the fury of human passion.

Chapter Twenty

∽

Remember that all things work for good for those who love God

St. Paul says that "all things work together for good to them that love God."[45] And as this maxim is used very often, when we are treating of the spiritual life, it is important that we should understand the meaning of it, that we should discern the reason of it and examine its consequences.

First, the apostle says *all things*. He excepts nothing. All the events of Providence, whether fortunate or unfortunate, everything that has to do with health or wealth or reputation; every condition of life, all the different interior states through which we may have to pass — desolations, dryness, disgust, weariness, temptations — all this is to be for the advantage of those who love God; and more than this — even our faults, even our sins.

We must be resolved never to offend God willfully; but if unfortunately we do offend Him, our very offenses, our very

---

[45] Rom. 8:28.

crimes, may be made use of for our advantage, if we really love God. We have only to remember David, we have only to remember St. Peter, whose sins served only to make them holier afterward — that is to say, more humble, more grateful to God, more full of love.

"All things work together for good." It is not a temporal good, not an earthly good. The Gospel warns us of that often enough. We are no longer under the dominion of the law, which promised temporal rewards to those who observed it; but we are under the rule of grace, which announces to those who wish to walk in the way of perfection only crosses and persecutions, and promises them only spiritual rewards. This is not difficult to understand: all things work together for the spiritual good of those who love God. Nevertheless, we must understand this good, not according to our own ideas, which are often mistaken, but according to the designs of God.

If there is one subject on which we are liable to be deceived, it is on all that concerns our spiritual interests. We form the most false ideas about it and often consider as hurtful to our soul that which is really most useful, and also as advantageous that which is really full of harm. Our self-love leads us on this matter into the strangest delusions. We must therefore believe — but with a belief that is born of faith and that does not rest on our own judgment — that our true good and our true advantage is found in the events of Divine Providence, and in all the different interior states through which God makes us pass, although often we cannot understand what God means to do with us and are quite ignorant as to what the end of these things is to be.

Remember that all things work for good

But all these divine arrangements are a good only for those who love God — that is to say, for those whose will is united and submissive to the will of God, those who in His service consider before all things the interests of God, the glory of God, and the accomplishment of His good pleasure, who are ready to sacrifice to Him everything without exception and who are persuaded that there is nothing better for a creature than to be lost in God and for God, because it is the only means of finding ourselves again in Him.

∾

God arranges everything for our good

All this is loving God truly, and with our whole heart. And this is what Jesus Christ meant when He said, "He that loves his life shall lose it; and he that loses his life for my sake shall find it in eternal life."[46] Whoever loves God in this manner is quite certain — and certain with an infallible certainty — that everything that God wills or permits with regard to him will be for his good, and even for his greatest good. He will not see it at the moment, because it is essential that he should not see it, and the sacrifices he has to make would not be accomplished if he did see it, but he will see it at the proper time. He will admire the wisdom and the infinite goodness of God in the wonderful way in which He leads the souls who belong to Him entirely. And he will see with astonishment that the very things that he feared would be for his hopeless ruin are those that have made his salvation assured.

[46] Cf. Luke 9:24; John 12:25.

It is not difficult to understand on what foundation St. Paul based his maxim.

God alone has the right idea of what sanctity is; He alone knows, and He alone has at His disposal, the means that can lead us to it. He alone also knows what is in the secret depths of our souls, our sentiments, our natural character, and the obstacles that are to be found there against our sanctity. He alone knows what secret motives will move us and how to bring us to the end that He intends for our sanctification without in any way constraining our free will. He knows what effect such and such an event, such and such a temptation, or such and such a trial will produce on us; and on His part, all is prepared so that it may have good success.

God has loved us from all eternity. He loved us first, before we could love Him, and there is nothing in us that is good, either in the order of nature or of grace, that He has not given to us. He loves us with a love that is infinitely wise, infinitely enlightened. He loves us not so much with regard to this present life, which is only passing away, only a time of trial, but with regard to the future life, which is our destination and our final end.

If, then, it is true that everything that happens here to the servants of God is overruled and arranged by infinite Love and Wisdom for their eternal happiness, it can be only through their own fault if the designs of God are not fulfilled. And if a single event happens that does not conduce to their spiritual advantage, it is most certainly through their want of love and trust, and their failing in conformity to the will of God. For, as long as they love God with a real, effective, and practical love, it is impossible for anything in the world to keep them back; on the contrary, everything will help to their advancement in perfection and will contribute to it.

∽

Abandon yourself to God's will

The consequences of this maxim of the apostle extend to everything and embrace every moment of life. The first is that if we wish to make sure of our salvation, as far as it is possible to do so, we must give ourselves up; we must abandon ourselves to God without reserve and forever. We must not wish to dispose of ourselves in anything. We must foresee nothing, arrange nothing, and determine nothing, except in the most entire dependence on God's good pleasure. We must not make one step or one single movement to take ourselves out of the actual situation where we are placed by the order of God. We must not even desire to come out of it, but we must allow ourselves, so to speak, to be drawn by the thread of Divine Providence and submit to every event as it happens. And as to what regards our innermost soul, we must remain quiet, without having any fears about the state in which God chooses us to be, without wishing for the change or the end of this state, however painful it may be to human nature.

The second conclusion to be drawn is that when we have contributed nothing to bring about a certain event, either exterior or interior, we may be quite sure that this event or this disposition of soul is the will of God for us, and consequently that it is the very best thing for us at the present moment. Thus, we ought to be very careful not to have a contrary opinion, nor to think that such and such a thing is unfortunate for us, or that it will do harm to our spiritual progress, or that God has forsaken us and will take no more care of us. We are very apt to judge in this manner when we find no more pleasure in our spiritual exercises, when we feel no longer that sweet peace and tranquility of soul that we once enjoyed, when we are attacked by violent temptations, when God withdraws from us all exterior support, even to the point of taking from us the guide in whom we had placed all our confidence. Then we think all is lost, because we see ourselves alone and without a guide.

But we are quite mistaken. God never acts so efficaciously as when He acts by Himself and when He takes away all external and sensible help; and His grace is never stronger and more real than when we have no sensible proof of it. And our cause for assurance is never greater than when we think we have lost all assurance.

But the chief thing is to know how to put our trust in God alone, in utter abandonment, in bare faith, without any reasonings or reflections, confiding ourselves and our interests entirely into the hands of God. It is then that, hoping against hope, we must say to ourselves, "Yes, I believe most firmly that all this will be for my good and that if I abandon myself entirely to God, I shall not be confounded."

The third conclusion to be drawn is that when we have once given ourselves to God, we must expect all kinds of sacrifices, and above all the sacrifice of our own will and our own judgment. We must expect to meet with many things in God's dealings with us that will strangely try our reason and will oblige us not to listen to its voice at all. We must expect all sorts of things that are most displeasing to our senses and most mortifying, all sorts of sufferings and humiliations, all sorts of interior and exterior disturbances that we could never foresee, which pass all our conceptions, and of which neither spiritual books nor the experience of others could ever give as the least idea. Finally, we must expect that God will carry fire and sword into the very depths of our hearts, that He will root out and burn up our self-love entirely, and that He will leave us nothing of our own.

This is undoubtedly very terrible to human nature; but the love of God, if it is what it ought to be, and if we allow it to do with us as He pleases, will dispose us for all these sacrifices and will not allow us to omit one. How could the maxim of St. Paul be true, if among all the things that God requires of a soul, there was a single one that was not for its spiritual and eternal advantage, and which therefore the soul thought it might refuse God? No. The apostle says *all things*. And that great and noble soul who, following the example of Jesus Christ, wished that he might even be accursed — without however any fault on his own part — for the sake of the salvation of the Jews, his brothers,[47] never thought that such a wish, so glorious to God, and so in conformity with the sentiments of Jesus Christ, could do otherwise than turn to his own advantage.

However great our sacrifices may be, they can never come up to those of our divine Master; and if His immolation of Himself, which was perfect, has procured for His sacred humanity a

[47] Rom. 9:3.

The Spiritual Life

glory and happiness above all that we can express or imagine,
we must believe with a firm faith that our immolation, imperfect as it may be, will procure for us a glory and happiness in
proportion to the extent and the generosity of the sacrifice.

∽

Fr. Jean Nicolas Grou
(1731-1803)

"If any man will come after me, let him deny himself, and take up his cross, and follow me."[48] Jean Nicolas Grou took these words of Christ to heart, bearing with peace and gentleness the crosses in his life and fixing his final gaze on the crucifix of our Savior.

Born in the diocese of Boulogne, France, Jean Grou entered the Jesuit novitiate at age fifteen and made his first vows at seventeen. When he took his final vows at Pont-à-Mousson, the Jesuits had already been suppressed in France, so Fr. Grou moved to Paris, where he took the name Leclaire and led a retired life devoted to study, religious duties, and writing.

When the French Revolution began, he planned to stay in Paris and continue his ministry in secret, but a holy Visitation nun whom he had befriended convinced him to seek refuge in England. There he became the spiritual director of the family

---

[48] Matt. 16:24.

with whom he stayed, and many revered him for his gentleness, wisdom, and experience in the spiritual life. It was in England that he learned that a great work of his, on which he spent fourteen years of research and writing, had been burned in Paris, but he bore the loss with remarkable peace of soul, accepting it as God's will.

Fr. Grou practiced strict poverty and showed lively faith, constant tranquility, and great humility, modesty, and zeal. Even in the last two years of his life, during which he suffered greatly from asthma and dropsy, he continued to hear confessions and to receive the sacraments with fervent devotion. Shortly before he died, he held a crucifix in his hands and exclaimed, "O my God, how sweet it is to die in Thine arms!"

Fr. Grou, in his life and in his writings, offers a powerful example of the holiness, peace, and happiness that come from denying ourselves and embracing the cross. Having walked the path of spiritual perfection and experienced its benefits even in this life, he continues to provide today's readers with the motivation and the practical spiritual direction to accept Christ's call to follow Him.

An Invitation

Reader, the book that you hold in your hands was published by Sophia Institute Press. Sophia Institute seeks to nurture the spiritual, moral, and cultural life of souls and to spread the Gospel of Christ in conformity with the authentic teachings of the Roman Catholic Church.

Our press fulfills this mission by offering translations, reprints, and new publications that afford readers a rich source of the enduring wisdom of mankind.

We also operate two popular online Catholic resources: CrisisMagazine.com and CatholicExchange.com.

Crisis Magazine provides insightful cultural analysis that arms readers with the arguments necessary for navigating the ideological and theological minefields of the day. *Catholic Exchange* provides world news from a Catholic perspective as well as daily devotionals and articles that will help you to grow in holiness and live a life consistent with the teachings of the Church.

In 2013, Sophia Institute launched Sophia Institute for Teachers to renew and rebuild Catholic culture through service to Catholic education. With the goal of nurturing the spiritual, moral, and cultural life of souls, and an abiding respect for the role and work of teachers, we strive to provide materials and programs that are at once enlightening to the mind and ennobling to the heart; faithful and complete, as well as useful and practical.

www.SophiaInstitute.com
www.CatholicExchange.com
www.CrisisMagazine.com
www.SophiaInstituteforTeachers.org

Sophia Institute Press® is a registered trademark of Sophia Institute. Sophia Institute is a tax-exempt institution as defined by the Internal Revenue Code, Section 501(c)(3). Tax I.D. 22-2548708.